Wines of Baja California
Touring and Tasting Mexico's Undiscovered Treasures

Ralph L. Amey

Wines of Baja California

Touring and Tasting Mexico's Undiscovered Treasures

Ralph L. Amey

The Wine Appreciation Guild
San Francisco

Wines of Baja California:

Touring and Tasting Mexico's Undiscovered Treasures

A Wine Appreciation Guild Book

Text and photos copyright © 2003 by Ralph Amey, PhD

Book Design: Diane Hume

Managing Editor: Bryan Imelli

Cartography: H. Hesse, Global Graphics

Circular Pre-columbian Mexican designs collected by Jorge Enciso.

Body text is Adobe Golden Type, with Adobe Poetica Chancery
and Dover Alouette and Artistik.

Library of Congress Cataloging-in-Publication Data

Text and Photos by Ralph Amey, PhD

Wines of Baja California: touring and tasting Mexico's undiscovered treasures/
1st ed.,

ISBN 1-891267-65-5

1. Wine and winemaking—Mexico—Baja California I. Ralph Amey, PhD

Library of Congress Control Number: 2003109112

Manufactured in the United States of America

The Wine Appreciation Guild Ltd
360 Swift Avenue
South San Francisco CA 94080
(650) 866-3020
www.wineappreciation.com

Contents

A Winemaker's Prologue

I look back 35 years to when I received my college degree at the University of Turin, Italy, returned to Baja and started working full time at our family winery and vineyard. At that time, there were only four commercial wineries in Baja: two in Tijuana and two in Ensenada, the latter being Bodegas de Santo Tomás and ours. The Mexican wine industry at that time was stagnant and focused on brandy production.

In 1976 our winery was sold to Domecq who was making large investments that brought new blood to the industry. But it wasn't until the mid '80s and early '90s that the second Renaissance began, with new wineries that not only continued to give credibility to Baja wines, but also strove to improve further the quality through revolutionary techniques that were being adopted by the international newcomers as well, such as the Australians, New Zealanders, South Africans, and Chileans.

During my childhood in the early '30s the industry experienced its first and most dynamic and enduring Renaissance, thanks to the right circumstances and the creative, aggressive and professional intervention of Enologist Esteban Ferro. In the thirties, about 90% of the grapes processed in Baja were grown in Southern California. However, between the late '30s and early '40s over 4,000 acres were planted to wine grapes in the Santo Tomás Valley. California provided equipment, and the redwood tanks now housed in the museum at Bodegas de Santo Tomás came from that period. These were still used during Dimitri Tchelistcheff's tenure to maintain Bodegas de Santo Tomás' reputation, thanks to his innovative techniques at that time. California was then the only supplier of corks, bottles and other supplies. During World War II the California Industry was in shambles and grape prices bottomed out. Thanks to this cheap source of grapes Bodegas de Santo Tomás became the leading winery, with a very strong financial position.

Years after, when Mexico closed the border to imported grapes, Bodegas de Santo Tomás, in an unprecedented move, financed the Guadalupe grain farmers with cuttings of French, Italian and Spanish varieties, brand new tractors, equipment and the technical advice needed to grow quality wine grapes. I remember when young, we would visit Guadalupe Valley during the winter rainy months having to cross several small creeks to get there from Ensenada, and being received by the grateful Molokan Russians, now viticulturists, to celebrate mass at their church.

Those were pioneering times. Now, 26 years in exile, I find myself consulting for Bodegas de Santo Tomás and I'm very proud to follow in my father's footsteps.

—Dr. Enrique Ferro
Temecula, CA
March, 2003

Preface

I t gives me great pleasure to see that someone has taken it upon himself to give the northern Baja region the recognition that it deserves for the production of fine wines.

Having worked in the region as Winemaker for fourteen years, and as Consultant for an additional twenty-two years, I can vouch for the historical, geographical, and technical accuracy of this book. It should be of great help to anyone wishing to enjoy the great wines of the region.

—Dimitri Tchelistcheff
Hawaii
February, 2003

Acknowledgements

It quickly became apparent how much I owe to my many generous and helpful friends, old and new, as I prepared this book. Jack Crane patiently demonstrated the important difference between the passive and active voice, and was a wonderful personal editor. Bev Crane revealed many of the tricks of Microsoft Word that had eluded me. Bob and Edie DeAvila and Marian Baldy generously shared their wisdom regarding the joys and pitfalls of first-time publishing. Thanks go to the wine tour participants, who joined me in visiting Baja's wineries, for their candid but encouraging comments. Special thanks to Diane McComber who spent much of one such trip annotating an early version of this text with helpful comments and questions. Catherine Speyer, an early admirer of the Guadalupe Valley, shared of her personal Baja knowledge while generously introducing me to many of the Valley's special people. Marc Bourreli, Gary Sehnert, Juaquin Leyva and Roy Miles have provided me with valuable insights into Baja California's wine industry. Without them, I could not have turned difficult tours and challenging tastings into triumphant moments. Al Doi, Jack Haeger and Jan Patten offered invaluable help regarding the book's design. Rondi Frankel's keen knowledge of Mexican history served well when she found errors of fact in an early manuscript version.

The people of Baja California have offered unwavering assistance and friendship. Camillo Magoni (master winemaker at L.A. Cetto) was particularly helpful, sharing his vast personal knowledge of the history of Baja's missions, the Guadalupe Valley and specifically his collection of vintage Guadalupe photos, some of which appear in this book. I have greatly appreciated his friendship and support throughout this project. Conversations with Hans Backhoff regarding his unique role as winemaker/partner at Mexico's first boutique winery (Monte Xanic) added to my understanding of the subject. Antoine Badan (Mogor-Badan) was exceptionally generous, arranging interviews and introducing me to his newer winemaker colleagues.

Of course little in this book could have been written without the support of all the other winemakers and owners of Baja's wineries. These wonderful, talented people have shared their vision of excellence for the region, and I thank them all for doing so. Further special thanks go to winemakers Fernando Martain, Victor Torres, Hugo D'Acosta, Jose Luis Durand, and David Bibayoff, as well as owners Fernando Favela, Eduardo Liceaga, and Don Miller. All these individuals share my deep appreciation for the natural beauty and traditional culture of these valleys, as well as a concern about their preservation.

I am deeply indebted to Dimitri Tchelistcheff and Enrique Ferro for contributing the Preface and Prologue respectively, as well as considerable personal knowledge concerning Baja's early wine history.

Two authors have published works that I have found especially valuable in writing my chapters on the history of winemaking and the valleys of Baja California. Peveril Meigs's seminal work on the "Dominican Mission Frontier of Lower

California" proved as relevant today as when it was first published in 1935. I found Héctor Arriola y Espinosa's "Los Apuntes de un Cofrade" (Notes of a Brotherhood Member) a warm and careful account of Mexico's wine history and of the founding in 1986 of La Cofradía del Vino de Baja California.

I acknowledge the considerable assistance provided by the Wine Makers Association of Baja California Mexico (Asociación de Vinicultores de Baja California Mexico) through their officers and members. I also appreciate being able to serve as a judge at the Vendimia's International Wine Competition. It allowed me the opportunity to taste Baja's best plus those of other countries in one incredible day.

I thank Elliott Mackey, publisher and his staff at the Wine Appreciation Guild for their invaluable professional assistance in guiding me through to a prompt publication.

Finally I owe the greatest thanks and appreciation to my spouse, Eunice Howe, without whose encouragement, and keen sense of editorial balance I would never have begun, let alone completed, this work.

—Ralph L. Amey
Plaza del Mar
Baja California
July, 2003

Introduction

I magine. I had been teaching and writing about wine for nearly twenty years before I discovered that Mexico has a burgeoning wine industry, and that it was just over the border in Baja California. For many of you that may not seem like much of an epiphany, but I was shocked. You see, I had grown up within three plus hours of the US/Mexico border, had enjoyed the pleasures of occasional trips to Tijuana, Rosarito Beach and Ensenada, and yet rarely had seen a Mexican wine listed on a restaurant menu in those cities. Even odder, I had never seen one for sale in any of the dozens of retail wine stores that I frequent in Los Angeles, nor had I encountered a U.S. review of a Mexican wine. Considering that I had devoured most newspaper wine articles published in Southern California over the past two decades, and faithfully read Wine Spectator and The Wine Enthusiast, not seeing a mention of Mexico's wines in any of them now amazed me.

We had just spent a weekend with some friends at their new home near San Quintín, some five hours south of the border, where we were reacquainting ourselves with the stunning beauty of Baja California's Pacific coast. We quickly succumbed. Soon we were looking for a site close enough to the border to make weekend stays a drivable practicality. As two college professors, we were looking for the quiet to write and the proximity to Los Angeles to permit returning to classes during the week. My only reluctance lay in a not so secret desire to live near a center of wine production, if not in sight of the vineyards, at least within a short drive from them. We found a great site, but I didn't see any vineyards. Further, I hadn't passed any lately, and I knew that premium wine grapes don't thrive where ice plant and salty sea foam happily co-mingle.

Not long afterward, one of our more wine-enlightened new Baja friends heard me expressing my frustration and said, "But there really are wineries in Baja California and they're not far away." I was aware of the old Bodegas de Santo Tomás winery, although I admit that I had no real idea where it was located. My lack of curiosity regarding this oldest winery in Baja sprang from tasting and dismissing several bottles of the rustic, nonvintage beverage from this winery some fifteen years earlier. Intended for early consumption, they had suffered the further indignity of sitting upright on retail shelves through at least one hot Baja summer.

The fact that our friend expressed his response in the plural immediately caught my attention. That evening I first heard of the Valle de Guadalupe, and that it was home to five or six (now almost a dozen) wineries, with two more located in Ensenada (yes, one was Santo Tomás). I wasted no time in visiting this valley, some two-thirds the size of Napa, with the name of the unofficial patron saint of Mexico. I discovered over the period of many visits that she had indeed blessed this area with a Mediterranean quality that has allowed it and its neighboring valleys of Santo Tomás and San Vicente to become the sources of over ninety percent of the premium table wines produced in Mexico.

The reasons for this best-kept secret are manifold and complex, and I mention some of them in an early chapter.

Certainly it doesn't help that beer has become Mexico's informal national drink, that the government has added wine to its list of luxury tax items (hopefully soon to be removed), and that the annual consumption of wine by all of Mexico measures slightly less than that of the inhabitants of the city of San Diego.

But I am happy to state that the Mexican wine industry is alive and growing, and nowhere more evident than in the area around Ensenada. Winemakers trained in more than seven different countries are producing exciting wines using modern viticultural methods, state of the art fermentation equipment and innovative winemaking techniques. Wineries are beginning to enjoy international recognition as their wines receive more gold, silver and bronze medals in respected competitions. Increasingly, restaurants in Mexico are featuring Mexican wines on their wine lists.

Recently, Baja's Tourism Secretariat announced plans to develop a "Grape Corridor" extending through the series of grape-growing valleys of Baja Norte. It is part of a larger plan to promote the wine industry by protecting local aquifers, cataloging the grapes, and establishing a council that would define and maintain standards of wine quality. These admirable objectives promise to develop a greater recognition and respect for Baja wines. However, the valley inhabitants who often view the land as a source of grapes, not as an opportunity for population growth and pollution, do not universally embrace such proposals, and the inevitable hotels, fast food stores, and housing that accompany them. To the relief of some and the disappointment of others, and unlike Chile, Argentina and Peru, foreign millions so far have failed to pour into the area to finance new vineyards and new wineries.

It is important to recognize that Baja is a distinct viticultural region, and its wines display their regional style no less than the wines of Napa, Bordeaux, Chablis and Rioja. The character of Baja wines frequently reveals itself in ripe fruit aromas, rich flavors, medium but distinct mid to forward tannins and mouth feel, and a clean, often lingering finish. The whites sometimes display subtle background minerality, especially those made from grapes grown at somewhat higher elevations and/or in the more granitic soils. The reds often give a sense of warm earthiness that blends well with the intense ripe fruit flavors displayed by the grapes grown here. Among the premium wines produced, the most frequently grown white grapes are Chardonnay, Sauvignon Blanc and Chenin Blanc, and the most popularly grown reds are Cabernet Sauvignon, Merlot, Cabernet Franc, Barbera, and Syrah. Smaller quantities of Viognier, Colombard, Petite Sirah, Grenache, Nebbiolo, Tempranillo and Zinfandel find their way into some of the bottles. In fact, many of the winemakers are proving to be enthusiastic and clever experimentalists, offering blends that are sometimes classic and sometimes creatively unique. Increasingly, Baja California's vintners are making wines of quality, as indicated by the growing number of medals and international awards they receive. Additionally, many are good value wines, offering excellent quality at competitive prices. Perhaps more importantly for us who consume them, these are becoming known as wines of pleasure, compatible with the wide variety of foods we enjoy eating. Finally, the valleys' Mediterranean climate provides an environment in which winemakers are finding opportunities for varietal diversity, not limited to just Chardonnay and Cabernet Sauvignon.

In this book I have attempted to provide you with a guide to the wines, wineries and winemakers of Baja, as well as the historical and geographical factors with which they are inextricably bound. Dimitri Tchelistcheff, son of Andre Tchelistcheff, and General Manager at Bodegas de Santo Tomás in the '60s, has generously contributed a thoughtful Preface. Dr. Enrique Ferro, son of Esteban Ferro, first Manager of Santo Tomás and initial importer of European grape vine cuttings to Baja, has donated a fascinating and personal Historical Prologue. A Spanish-English glossary of terms has been included to assist you in interpreting wine labels. Our trek begins in earnest with a chapter that briefly spans the history of the Mexican wine industry, while placing Baja's vitivinicultural role in context. A section on northern Baja's important Valle de Guadalupe, and one on the smaller nearby valleys follow. These three sections also describe the important role that missions played in the wine grape industry. If your interest lies with the wineries themselves you can turn directly to the following sections where each winery and its wines are profiled. I have also included suggestions for food items that I have found particularly compatible with each wine. I encourage you however, to experiment and try these wines with some of your own favorite foods. Subsequent sections include suggestions for places to eat, rest, and where to read more on the subject.

To enjoy a delicious wine is truly a pleasure, but to experience it along with the beauty of the land in which the grapes were nurtured and where the wine was created then becomes a revelation. Whether discovering this part of Baja for the first time, or tasting what is new in a familiar landscape, I hope that the contents of this book will help make your visit a special one.

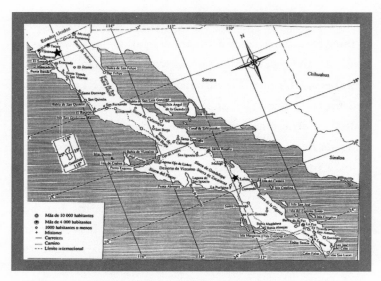

Early map of Baja California. The Transpeninsular Highway wanders from Tijuana to Cabo San Lucas, a distance of 1,059 miles (1,704 km). The first wine grapes in Baja California were planted at Misión San Javier near Loreto (see star at latitude 26º) by Padre Juan de Ugarte ca. 1701. Today Mexico's major wines are made in Baja Norte near Ensenada.

Part 1

History & The Valleys

A selection of wines produced in Baja California. Because most labels are in Spanish, understanding the equivalent English terms, if one is not fluent in the former, helps to identify the wine's style and character. (For list of terms in Spanish please see appendix.)

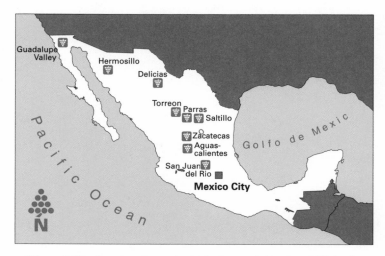

Map of Mexico showing principal vineyard districts. With the exception of Baja Norte, most of the harvest goes towards the production of table grapes or brandy. (Courtesy: Global Graphics)

Chapter 1

A Brief History of
Winemaking in Mexico

The Grape

Upon completing their arduous sea journey from Spain to Cuba, and eventual arrival on the coast of Mexico in 1519, a strange and unfamiliar landscape greeted Hernán Cortés and his thirsty Conquistadores. Instead of their familiar Spanish they found wild vines of the indigenous grapes of New Spain. Needless to say, this was a desperate situation for the Spanish invaders, who were accustomed to tasty wine as a beverage for washing down their meals, and for the Catholic emissaries who used it in their celebration of the Mass. Obviously something had to be done and soon. Here the story becomes a bit hazy. One account has the Spanish sailors eating the raisins that they brought with them, and spitting the seeds out where they sprouted as grape vines. Another had the enterprising Jesuit missionaries recognize a solution to their dilemma and deliberately planting the raisin seeds and cultivating the resulting vines. A third story, prob-ably apocryphal, found Cortés' father sending the new gover-

9

nor some vine cuttings from Spain, which Cortés promptly planted. Whatever actually happened, the details were forever lost in the enthusiasm to find gold and to convert the natives to Christianity.

However one thing is certain: the grapes being cultivated at that time in faraway Spain, whether for eating or fermenting to wine, were of the European species *Vitis vinifera* vastly different than those growing in Mexico and the Americas. In the early sixteenth century, the vinicultural skills of Spain's winemakers lay largely in making sherry, where relatively simple grapes could be made into a stable, high alcohol beverage. Their techniques for making ordinary table wine, though, had changed little from those of the Romans. Although they used barrels extensively for crushing, fermentation and storage, spoilage was a problem, and they seldom considered long-term aging as practical. When barrels were unavailable, they used animal skins as containers. These imparted other undesirable aromas and flavors to the wine. Further, up to that point Spaniards had not bothered to identify many of the grape varieties that they were growing. Those with higher sugar content were used both as table grapes and as sweet wines, the sugar or resultant high alcohol improving their otherwise limited flavor and stability. According to Hugh Johnson in *Vintage: The Story of Wine* Spain's most popular export wines of that time went by local and regional names such as "Ryvere," "Ribadavia," "Osoye," and "Bastardo," and were characteristically not the best wines. The nature of these "shipping wines" was probably never fully known nor worried about since the many little producers each may have had their own vineyard or source, probably a field blend of available grapes. In fact, as trade with New Spain later improved, among the earliest items to be shipped from Spanish ports were olive oil and wine, two of Spain's biggest European trade products. Unfortunately, this plan to increase their profitable trade with the Americas proved to be largely a disaster. The long, often hot journey turned the oil rancid and the wine became vinegar.

Although there are no official records to support it, some feel that the grape that serendipitously traveled in some form or another to New Spain was the Monica, an unassuming, relatively tasteless pale red grape then grown in Spain and Sardinia. The latter island now is the sole source of this grape, its cultivation in Spain having disappeared long ago. Whatever the grape variety, it soon began to be planted with the enthusiasm that only a religiously fervent and thirsty community could display.

As Spain's appointed governor of this land from 1521 to 1527, Cortés dictated the mining and farming practices of the day. He is said to have insisted that all ships sailing from Spain and the Canary Islands to Vera Cruz should bring cuttings, plants and seeds. By then, some of these must have been grape cuttings. Then, in 1524 he ordered every Spaniard that held a *repartimiento* (a land grant including native Indians to work the land) to plant, annually for five years, 10 grapevines per Indian. About 5,000 grape vines were thus planted. Whether by importation or by eventual hybridization among species from Spain or with a native non-*vinifera* grape, the local grape industry seems to have settled on a species that came to be called the Criolla (loosely translated as "New World scion of an Old World parent, adapted to the new condition"). Mission inhabitants and eventually all Mexicans willingly snacked on this sturdy, low-colored, low-acid, but high-yield (greater than six tons per acre) grape that also could be turned into a fairly neutral-flavored sweet table wine. Later, it was also used in the production of brandy. The

Criolla formed the basis of America's first wine production and helped quench the thirst of the new Spanish inhabitants. Much later, as the Mission grape, it initiated the start of a new industry in California, but not before it struggled to survive in its trek across mainland Mexico and into Baja California.

Early Wine Development

By 1554 winegrowing had become well established at haciendas as far west as Michoacán. The first commercial vineyard *(bodega vinícola)* in Mexico was probably planted in 1593 by a Spanish captain named Francisco de Urdiñola at Parras de la Fuente in Coahuila, 500 miles north of Mexico City. The name Parra means, "vine," and Parras is still a center of viticulture, with the plantation of Don Francisco, which is located between Monterrey and Torreon, always producing grapes. Parras, the oldest town in northern Mexico, is located in the state of Coahuila de Zaragoza, adjoining the U.S. border just below Texas. Coahuila ("naked snake") is largely a vast rolling plateau with a hot and arid climate. The grapes grown there today go largely into the production of brandy and blended jug wines and require irrigation to provide the high yields needed for such products. Curiously, so successful was this 16th century enterprise that in 1595 Spain's King Philip II issued an edict from Madrid that totally prohibited new plantings or replacement of vines in Mexico in order to protect Spain's home wine market.

In 1597 Don Lorenzo Garcia rediscovered the site of the earliest American native wine production at Santa Maria de las Parras, obtained ownership through a Royal Land Grant and named it the San Lorenzo Vineyards and Winery. Viceroys maintained the crown's command throughout the following several centuries, and wine remained a Spanish monopoly. But winemaking continued despite the distant laws, though without any records of the quantities made.

Thus it was from Mexico, not Europe that during the sixteenth century winemaking reportedly spread with the help of Jesuit missionaries to Peru, Chile and Argentina, and in the eighteenth century to parts of western United States. In fact, today, the largest acreage of Criolla is still found in Argentina, where it is known as the Criolla Chica. Chile continues to produce wine from the Pais, believed to be a variant of Criolla, and in Peru one can find a related version called the Negra Corriente. As the missionaries carried cuttings of this sturdy grape along with them on their mission-founding westward travels, the Criolla assumed the more comfortable name of the Misión or Mission grape. However it took almost one hundred years more before the Jesuit missionary Father Juan Ugarte, known as the grandfather of Mexican viticulture, found his way to Baja California and planted at nearby Mission San Javier the first pure or hybrid *Vitis vinifera* grape. The first Baja mission was founded some five hundred miles south of the California border at Loreto in 1697, and Father Ugarte arrived at his new assignment soon afterward. He is credited with planting the first vineyard there around 1701. Yet it took almost another three-quarters of a century before Franciscan Friar Junipero Serra carried the Mission grape across the border into California, and fifty-four years more for him to complete the mission trail by founding the twenty-first California mission in the northern town of Sonoma.

In 1810, Padre Miguel Hidalgo, a strong advocate of native independence, dared to oppose the Spanish laws and led the revolution against Spain. One of his goals was to end the

Spanish wine monopoly and to renew viticulture in Mexico. As parish priest in his village of Dolores, in mainland Mexico, Hidalgo taught the natives how to grow and crush grapes and to make wine. Not surprisingly he antagonized the authorities that repeatedly came and tore out his vines. Unfortunately, with the successful completion of the uprising eleven years later, and the subsequent execution of Hidalgo, the nascent Mexican wine industry was unable to position itself for further development. Much later, the continued preference of the Mexican ruling class for French wines gave little opportunity for Mexico's wine industry to reestablish itself.

The First "Modern" Mexican Wineries

In 1870 Don Evaristo Madero acquired the old Bodegas San Lorenzo and promptly renamed it Casa Madero. Claiming a tradition of nearly 300 years and ownership of the oldest winery and vineyards in the American continent, Madero set about to upgrade his facility by importing from Europe cuttings of various *Vitis vinifera* grapes. The effort paid off, for his wines soon won numerous medals and received international recognition. Unfortunately, the vineyards eventually were lost to phylloxera and the winery gradually fell into disuse until the vines were replanted on resistant rootstock in 1962. It now claims the first regional appellation in Mexico (Valle de Parras), and produces a selection of wines from their *Vitis vinifera* plantings. With an annual production of 350,000 cases, up until recently almost all of it has been shipped overseas, little being drunk at home. As they improve the quality of their wines, however, this is changing. They are winning more awards, they now distribute nationally, and their *reserva* wines are recognized for their high quality.

As noted, development was slow, and during the first seventy years of independence, only three new wineries were established—the Bodegas Ferriño in Coahuila in 1860, the Bodegas San Luis Rey in Guanajuato in 1870, and the Bodegas de Santo Tomás in Baja California in 1888. A little clarification is probably helpful here. Casa Madera is acknowledged as the oldest commercial winery in Mexico. However, because of their problems with phylloxera at the beginning of the 20th century, production ceased for a while; thus it is not the oldest *continuing* commercial winery. That honor goes to Bodegas Ferriño. The Bodegas San Luis Rey stopped production sometime in the 1900's. As will be noted later, Santo Tomás was the first, and remains the oldest continually operating winery in Baja California, and is the second oldest holding this claim in Mexico.

For over three hundred years the Criolla/Mission grape continued to be distributed and vinified throughout Mexico. Being a prolific and vigorous vine, the Mission survived and dominated most of Mexico's vineyards. Although Mexico is not a significant source of the grape today, the extensive plantings in Chile and Argentina are sufficient to rank it 6th overall worldwide and 3rd among reds. Although claimed by some sources to be partly responsible for the low quality of California table wines prior to 1880, it was still the fourth ranking grape grown in the Golden State in 1944, planted to 10,906 acres. By 1976 it had dropped to sixteenth in rank and plantings had shrunk to about 5,000 acres. Surprisingly, as recently as 1994 California still had 1,060 acres (424 hectares) planted to the Mission, and the University of California at Davis Rootstalk Program currently lists nine selections of Mission in their library. Although Jancis Robinson in her 1996 book, *Vines, Grapes & Wines,* notes that plantings were "mainly in southern California and nearly half of them in San Bernardino County," these have been used largely as a blending source (Mondavi and Gallo used them in their bulk wine production). Several small wineries in the Sierra foothills (Malvadino, Shenandoah, and Story wineries) still produce Mission-based wines, largely for historical interest.

Help from California

By the end of the nineteenth century, however, the first large-scale experiments with good European vine stocks were being made. In 1889, James Concannon, seeking more capital for his newly founded Concannon Vineyard and Winery in Livermore, California, convinced Mexico's new dictator-president, Porfirio Díaz, that viticulture could be developed on a commercial quality basis, and that Concannon was the person to do it. Díaz granted him a concession to introduce better wine grapes into Mexico. From Livermore, where Concannon was planting his own new vineyard with French varieties, thousands of cuttings were sent to haciendas throughout northern Mexico, along with pamphlets in Spanish on grape cultural methods. Concannon completed his project six years later and returned to California.

In 1910, the resulting winemaking boom attracted Antonio Perelli-Minetti to Mexico. Perelli had just lost a fortune in a wine venture in San Francisco and was looking for an opportunity to recoup his losses. With President Díaz's encouragement, and the rejoinder that "The sky's the limit here," Perelli imported more cuttings from California and planted them on the rancho of Felipe Càrdenas near Torréon. Càrdenas was the brother of a former governor of the early vineyard center of Coahuila, and early relative of a later Mexican president and of the recent mayor of Mexico City. The cuttings included Zinfandel, Petite Sirah, Malaga, and

Flame Tokay, with which he created a 900-acre vineyard, the largest in Mexico at that time.

Timing once again proved awkward, for that very year marked the Revolution of 1910, exactly 100 years after the Hidalgo uprising. Except for the few vineyards temporarily protected by the bandit leader and Mexican general Pancho Villa, most of Mexico's old and new vineyards were neglected or destroyed during the long and bloody war. In 1916 Perelli quit in frustration and returned to California. After the Revolution, Perelli did return to Mexico and eventually assisted some of the emerging wineries.

Mexico's Modernization

Only in the period of stability following the 1940's did a modern winemaking industry begin to emerge, helped by a rigorous protectionism encouraged by the long-ruling PRI *(Partido Revolucionario Institucional)* political party. After the Second World War, the Mexican government stimulated the planting of vineyards by quadrupling the tariffs on European wines and by putting quota restrictions on wine imports. Suddenly, French, Spanish, and California wines cost five times as much as Mexican wines. As Mexican grape supplies increased, European and American companies began to build their own plants in Mexico. Although primarily to make brandy instead of wine, companies such as Pedro Domecq, Martell Cognac, Seagram and Osborne established themselves as major consumers of Mexican grapes.

In four and a half decades, the area planted to vineyards in Mexico grew more than thirty-fold, from 4,000 acres (1,600 hectares) in 1939 to 117,000 acres (47,000 hectares) in 1985. Perhaps a more significant measure of growth is in terms of wine production figures. Many Mexican wineries suffered major setbacks in 1982 when government deregulation of imports brought heavy competition from cheap, low-quality imported wines. This led to many estates being forced out of business and a decrease in overall vineyard acreage and wine production in 1986-90. It is important also to note that only about ten percent of wine production still goes into table wine; the other 90 percent is used in brandy production. From 1992 to 1995 growth continued with current production reported at more than 2.7 million hectares (a 12 percent growth rate).

The per capita wine consumption of Mexico is only 1/34th the consumption in the United States, a more troubling statistic for the domestic wineries. As a country, it ranks virtually at the bottom of the list of major and minor wine consuming countries of the world. To place this in some perspective, consider that Mexico's annual national consumption is slightly less than that of the inhabitants of San Diego, a California city just across the border from Tijuana. Leon Adams, in his classic book entitled *The Wines of America* (1985), listed four reasons for the Mexican reluctance to consume wine, and vestiges of all four continue to be relevant today:

- Despite the wine-friendly Mexican cuisine, three major competitors are: beer, soft drinks, and pulque. The latter is an ancient Aztec drink fermented to about 4-6 percent alcohol from the juice of the cactus-like maguey plant (source of tequila and mescal through distillation). Millions of gallons of pulque are sold annually, and more is home-brewed for personal consumption.
- The Mexican government for many years misunderstood the role of table wine as a mealtime beverage and lumped it with distilled spirits. For example, beer has been promoted as "the beverage of moderation." Until

recently licenses to sell wine were costly and difficult to obtain. Fortunately, this has changed, and restaurants can now obtain wine licenses as easily and inexpensively as one for beer. Frustratingly, a significant tax has been placed on table wine, putting it out of reach of many Mexican households. In fact, those few Mexican wines that currently are exported to the United States cost less there than in Mexico.

- Up until recently, most wine has been bought and consumed by wealthy and upper-class people in Mexico to serve on special occasions. For many Mexicans that has meant buying expensive imported brands from France and Spain. For over four-and-a-half centuries, many of the wealthy and upper class of Mexico have taken the position that no native product or custom can equal its counterpart in Europe, from which (they perceive) civilization came to the New World. This attitude is known in Mexico as *malinchismo.* This term derives from La Malinche, given to an Indian girl originally named Malintzín, later held captive by a local Tabascan chief, and baptized Doña Marina when given to Cortés as a gift. The talented Doña Marina served as interpreter, mistress and slave of Cortés, guiding him in his conquest of Moctezuma's Aztec empire. For betraying her race, legend states that she was condemned to wander forever in tears and agony beneath a lake by day and through the country by night. *Malinchista* became the term applied to people who show a preference for customs other than Mexican. Fortunately, this attitude is gradually changing as Mexican wines improve.

- Until recently, very few restaurants in Mexico included the domestic product on their wine lists. Although a difficult barrier to overcome, in 1965 the Government passed laws that encouraged greater restaurant use of Mexican wines. More recently, however, a new tax has been imposed that increases the price of all alcoholic drinks in restaurants.

Although these actions seem at times to be at cross-purposes, it is possible to see progress, albeit slow. As the quality of these wines rises we are seeing a reduction in *malinchismo* and an increase in acceptance of Mexican wines on restaurant wine lists.

Early Baja Winemaking

It is fitting that our journey through Mexico's wine industry brings us at last to the Far West and the wineries of Northern Baja California (Baja Norte). As noted earlier, the Mission grape came to Baja soon after the first peninsular mission was founded at Loreto in 1697. Winemaking techniques remained primitive, with cowhides used as containers in the fermentation of the grapes.

As mainland wineries turned to brandy as their cash cow, table wine production figures stagnated. The pioneering frontier spirit led to the founding in 1888 of Baja California's first commercial winery, near the site of the former Mission Santo Tomás de Aquino. Spanish missionaries founded the latter in 1791 in what is today the Valle de Santo Tomás, approximately 45 Km (30 mi) south of Ensenada, the principal port in northern Baja. In those days the missionaries made wine for Mass and sold the surplus to locals. In 1857, however, the Mexican government expropriated all church property. Don Loreto Amador, a local entrepreneur from the village of Santo Tomás, bought the mission lands, and soon after acquired its

Cowhide used for fermenting grapes. Located at Misión San Javier, southwest of Loreto. (Courtesy: C. Magoni)

Ancient vine possibly planted in the early 18th century at Misión San Javier. (Courtesy: C. Magoni)

Stone container, carved from one piece, for making and storing wine. At Misión San Francisco Borja de Adác, east of the bay (Bahía) of Viscaíno. Probably carved during the time of the Jesuits with the founding of the mission in 1759. (Courtesy: C. Magoni)

vineyards. In turn, he renamed the property "Rancho de los Dolores," and began his own commercial wine production. This operation must have been pretty successful for it lasted 31 years, until Don Francisco de Andonegui and Don Miguel Ormart, two Ensenada businessmen, bought it in 1888. From this purchase they founded Bodegas de Santo Tomás. Initially wine was bulk produced and shipped to the surrounding small towns and villages (It is rumored that some even found its way across the border into the San Diego area of Southern California). But in 1931 the winery operations, now under the management of Esteban Ferro, a viniculturist trained in Italy, were moved to Ensenada, where Santo Tomás could take advantage of the busy city's transportation network and port facilities. In 1932 the winery was purchased by General Abelardo Rodríguez, then governor of Baja Norte and later president of Mexico. It soon was moved to a larger, new site downtown, where the first bottling took place in 1939 under the direction of Ferro. Cuttings of Italian varietals from his native Piedmont and French varietals acquired from Livermore's Wente Bros. Winery provided a quantum leap up in quality over the Mission grapes being vinified up to that time.

Meanwhile, vineyards planted as early as the late 1800's in the Valle de Guadalupe to the northeast of Ensenada

1924 photo of Molokan couple hand harvesting grapes in Valle de Guadalupe. (Courtesy: C. Magoni)

1930 photo of Molokan farmer plowing his vineyard. (Courtesy: C. Magoni)

continued to provide table grapes for the valley's agrarian inhabitants. By 1943 Santo Tomás' Manager and Enologist, Esteban Ferro, was purchasing a variety of largely white grapes from valley growers, as well as grapes from farmers in the United States to meet the winery's expanding wine production needs. By 1946 Ferro also had planted extensive holdings of red Italian varieties. This important region has now become the focal point of Baja's premium wine production, and its historical development has been given its own chapter in this book (see "Valle de Guadalupe").

Modern Baja Begins

A further commitment to quality improvement at Santo Tomás was made in 1962 when the winery hired Dimitri Tchelistcheff as technical director. His father André was the genius behind the great Private Reserve wines of Beaulieu Vineyard. At Dimitri's request some of the Valle de Santo Tomás vineyards were replanted with Cabernet, Pinot Noir, Riesling, Chenin Blanc and Chardonnay; cold fermentation of whites was introduced, and Tchelistcheff is credited with producing Baja's first sparkling wines. In 1977 Tchelistcheff

A view of modern Valle de Guadalupe, looking southward from above L.A. Cetto. Note the bullring in right foreground.

left Santo Tomás and returned to California where he began to consult for other wineries.

Now it's back to its roots, with a new, $6 million winery recently completed adjacent to their vineyards in the Valle de Santo Tomás. The dramatic state-of-the-art facility features gravity-flow wine transfer, and automated temperature and humidity control. The current Ensenada facility will be devoted to the winery's expanded sparkling wine production and serve as its bottling plant, as well as provide a popular tourist attraction. Elias Pando, a wine-importing firm and market conglomerate headquartered in Mexico City, purchased Santo Tomás in 1968.

Located a few kilometers beyond the village of Francisco Zarco in the Valle de Guadalupe is the impressive winery founded in 1972 by Pedro Domecq, the huge brandy conglomerate. Initially named Vides del Guadalupe, it is now known as Casa Pedro Domecq. The founding of Vinicola L.A. Cetto, an even larger winery directly across from Domecq, soon followed this. Founder Luis Angel Cetto was also Domecq's manager for several years and his family still retains a major financial interest in Domecq. Cetto came to Guadalupe from Italy in 1923 and eventually ended up in Tijuana where he made bulk wine at his Productos de Uva cellar. Under the direction of his son, the winery and its holdings have grown into the largest wine producer in Mexico. Cetto's winemaker, Camillo Magoni, earned his enology degree in northern Italy where he studied the Nebbiolo grape. He was hired by Señor Cetto over thirty years ago initially to oversee winemaking operations at Domecq, and later moved to the Cetto facility where he continues as their Director of Winemaking. In the 70's Magoni identified a thousand hectares (~2500 acres) in the Valle de Guadalupe for planting to French and Italian varieties. Today, wines made from those plantings provide some of the super premium offerings of these two wineries.

Modern Baja Continues

The last dozen years have seen the emergence of several new wineries in this area, including Ensenada's other urban winery Cavas Valmar (1983), and an increasing number of Valle de Guadalupe-based facilities. Among the latter are (in order of founding): Vinos Bibayoff (1970s), San Antonio (now owned by Santo Tomás) (1986), Mogor-Badan (1987), Monte Xanic (1988), Chateau Camou (1991), Viña de Liceaga (1993), Casa de Piedra (1997), Adobe Guadalupe (2001), Rincon de Guadalupe (2001), and Vinisterra S.A. de C.V. (2002). With ninety percent of Mexico's table wines now being produced in Northern Baja, it is apparent that these and perhaps even newer neighbors will play major roles in the emerging wines of Mexico.

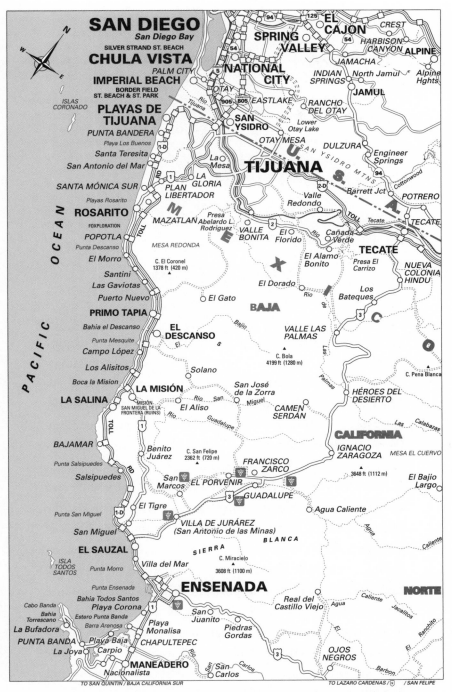

Map of the area between Tijuana, Tecate and Ensenada, indicating the various ways to reach the Valle de Guadalupe. (Courtesy: Global Graphics)

Chapter 2

Getting There

Reaching the wine country of Baja California is quite simple. There are actually three border crossings: Tijuana (San Ysidro), Tecate and Otay Mesa. Although Otay Mesa is less crowded, most of you will probably enter Mexico either through Tijuana or Tecate, since Otay Mesa is less direct. Below I'll describe the other two approaches.

But beforehand, I strongly recommend that you do two things. First, purchase a copy of the *Baja California* book and the companion *Baja California* map from the Automobile Club of Southern California. These offer valuable information on how to make your international visit particularly enjoyable. Secondly, you will need to purchase Mexico auto insurance before crossing the border. You can obtain it through the Automobile Club, or at one of the many drive-up kiosks labeled "Mexican Insurance" that are located at most freeway off-ramps as you approach the border. It's inexpensive and you pay only for as many days as you plan to spend in Baja.

From Tijuana

Both U.S. Interstate Highways 5 and 805 from San Diego lead directly south to the international border. The San Ysidro-Tijuana border crossing is open 24 hours. About a quarter mile before the border, the road broadens into a series of lanes. They can be filled with vehicles, or not, depending on the time of day. When the border is busy, each car seems to be driven by somebody who needs to cut in front of you to get to your gate first. In reality, all lanes move equally fast, and concrete dividers now make such road race antics difficult. When entering Mexico through one of the several open gates, most travelers receive a green light (*passe*) and are waved through. For a few, randomly chosen it is rumored, the light turns red, and the travelers are motioned to one side. If this happens to you, a uniformed officer will greet you, glance into your car and ask where you are going. Smile, tell him that you are going to Ensenada, and you will be waved back into bustling traffic. Follow the many overhead signs marked "Ensenada Toll Road" (*Cuota* means "toll"), or "Rosarito/ Ensenada/ Scenic Road."

Although this first experience of Tijuana is seemingly hectic, attention to the signs leads you directly to Mexico Highway 1-D. This bypasses Tijuana's most congested streets and instead parallels the infamous border. (If your passengers look carefully to their right, they can spot U.S. border patrol vehicles with officers watching for illegal crossings).

In about four miles you follow a broad curve south and head past the off-ramp to Playas de Tijuana, a suburb populated by many of Tijuana's professionals. Here you have your first good view of Baja's Pacific coast, and dominating the shoreline on your right is the aptly named Bullring-by-the-Sea.

A half-mile further, you reach the first of three toll stations, or *"Cuotas,"* encountered between Tijuana and Ensenada (toll varies with the current conversion rate, but is posted in both dollars and pesos). Here officially begins Mexico's Toll Highway 1-D, which in a little less than one and a half hours (62 miles, 100 kilometers) will bring you to the junction with Highway 3, the southern entrance to Baja's wine country. This excellent divided highway is well maintained, and offers the safest, shortest route to Ensenada. The drive south provides spectacular views of the Pacific coastline, sometimes near sea level, and sometimes at dizzying (but safe) heights above the largely undeveloped land north of Ensenada. At regular intervals, the distance from Tijuana is posted in kilometers (divide by three, multiply by 2 to get it in miles).

Along the Way

At the Km 19 marker is *Real del Mar*, a resort complex run by Marriott with an excellent golf course and one of Tijuana's hottest new restaurants, *Rincón San Román*. Here French-trained Chef Martin San Román prepares outstanding Mexican-French cuisine in a romantic upstairs setting. Importantly, chef San Román loves wine, and Baja's best appear on his wine list.

At 28 and 33.5 Kms respectively, are off ramps for the north (*norte*) and south (*sud*) ends of Rosarito, a popular resort for tourists and students on Spring Break. It's also a great place to shop for quality Mexican items for the home or for that special gift. The 100-plus restaurants guarantee a meal to satisfy everyone's taste.

As you leave Rosarito, you encounter the second toll station at Km 35.

At about Km 40, on the right is the Titanic Museum and Foxploration, a part of 20ᵗʰ Century Fox Studios that was built to shoot most of this blockbuster film. For those who love Hollywood and are passing when it's open, this is a must stop. For the rest, keep moving.

Near Km 52 is the exit for Lobster Village. If you get off you will meet the "free road," a paved but two-lane road parallel to the highway, at the bottom of the off ramp. Turn left, drive a couple miles further south, and watch for a large arch on the right (where the crowd is). Technically named *Puerto Nuevo*, the popular Lobster Village claims over thirty restaurants specializing in grilled lobster at low prices. Although the menus are much the same, each visitor has a favorite place, and returns to it again and again.

Once back on the toll road (yes, there is an on-ramp farther south of Lobster Village, across from a Pemex station) you pass several small communities. At Km 64 is the exit for Hotels *La Misión* and *La Fonda*, each featuring a popular Mexican restaurant.

The foggy shore at low tide, south of Rosarito near Km 64.

31

La Salina ("Salt Marsh") is a developing marina, where early inhabitants mined for salt. Now it's where you can build a house and dock your own yacht outside the front door. It's near Km 72.

To your right at Km 76 is *Bajamar*, a large rambling resort development. The excellent seaside golf course offers the golfer spectacular ocean views while being challenged to beat par. The hotel serves a delicious Sunday brunch.

At Km 82 is the off-ramp for *El Mirador* ("Viewpoint"). Appropriately named, and well worth a stop, the sweeping view from the overlook behind the restaurant is stunning, as you gaze at the southern coastline. The "guard rail" is disturbingly low, so take care, but a cautious glance downward from several hundred feet above the rocky shore is also awesome. Check out the car wrecks at the bottom, possible evidence of the earlier popularity of this site as one for playing "car chicken." If you choose not to stop, at least slow down for the sharp turn here, and alert your passengers to enjoy the great view (assuming no coastal fog) as you descend (*Area de Descansco*).

The final toll station is at Km 97, along with a state-run Tourist Information booth located just south of the gate, on the right-hand side.

At this point you drive along a toll-free, divided road while passing through a modestly populated, commercial-industrial strip. Eventually Highway 1 passes through *El Sausal*, a sprawling community that is home to a fish cannery. If you were to continue farther, you would find trailer parks, motels and several excellent hotels and restaurants, prior to entering the port of Ensenada.

However, just a mile and a half beyond the tollgate you reach a looping overhead off-ramp labeled "Tecate 3." Pass under the bridge, immediately turn right and begin your trek into Baja's wine country.

From Tecate

Those who approach Baja from the east have a more straight-forward, albeit geographically different journey to the wine country. This also offers an alternative route for departure from the Valle de Guadalupe and return to the United States. The fact is, Tecate is much less congested on either side of the international border, and thus crossing can be much faster than at San Ysidro. In contrast to the latter's twenty-four hour open-gate policy, however, the border at Tecate only remains open from 6:00 am to midnight daily. Because of the more relaxed traffic here, you are even less likely to be stopped on crossing into Mexico and entering the friendly town of Tecate.

If you have time, stop at *Parque Hidalgo*, the central tree-shaded plaza. This is a worthwhile place to pause and buy an ice cream (*hilado*) cone or popsicle (*paleta*) or slushy (*rapado*) from one of the numerous stand-owners or ice cream stores (*neverias*). The latter are often part of the popular *La Michoacana* ice cream chain that displays easily recognized rainbow-striped signs. The product is quite safe to eat. Try one of the more unusual and delicious flavors not likely found in the U.S., such as "tamarind, cactus/cheese or avocado" ice cream, or "gardenia petal or pineapple/chile pepper" popsicles. The *Parque* is just to your left as Calle Cardenas (the street on which you entered Tecate) intersects Avenida Juarez. This is Highway 2, the Tijuana-Mexicali expressway. You will also find a State Tourism office (SECTUR) on the south side of the plaza.

The numerous "to Hwy 3" signs will lead you around *Parque Hidalgo* and south onto Calle Ortiz Rubio.

Located just west of the city is Rancho La Puerta, a physical fitness spa-resort serving strictly vegetarian meals, and frequented by the rich and famous since 1940.

With more available free time, you might want to tour the huge Cuauhtémoc Brewery, best known as the home of Tecate beer. Free tours are available every day except Sunday, at 11:00 a.m. and 3 p.m., with the beer garden open from 10 a.m. to 5:30 p.m. Tuesday through Saturday. To get there, drive one block south of the plaza, on Calle Ortiz and turn right on Avenida Hidalgo. The brewery is a short distance between Calle Elías and Calle Carranza on the left. Look for the tower-like stainless-steel vats and red-and-white billboard. You can't miss it.

Along the Way

Back on Calle Ortiz Rubio, you now leave Tecate and head south on Highway 3. Expect to reach the north end of the Valle de Guadalupe, about 45 miles distant, in approximately one hour. The distance markers indicate the number of kilometers from Tecate. The northern part of this sparsely populated section of Baja will remind you of Southern California's backcountry, with rolling hills, cattle ranches, fruit and olive orchards.

At Km 10.5 you pass the low profile Rancho Tecate Resort and Country Club, a popular resort that offers tennis, swimming and golf, and definitely non-vegetarian meals. Built on the site of a turn-of-the-century winery, it still features a two-story-tall thirty-foot-wide original oak barrel that now serves as the hacienda's stairwell.

Another twelve meandering and hot miles through vineyards used in producing lesser bulk wine, you pass Km 28 and enter the Valle de las Palmas. This is an agricultural community where you can buy food at one of the roadside stores, and fill your car at a Pemex station. Some wine is made here, largely Chenin Blanc, although until recently the growers sold their grapes to wineries in Guadalupe and Ensenada. From here you gradually begin to climb through undeveloped farmland and rugged hills toward a cooler, higher elevation.

At Km 50 you pass through the village of El Testerazo. Note the impressive rocky peaks to the west, some of which are 3000 to 4200 feet in elevation.

From here it's a short run to Km 74.5, and the gates of Domecq and L.A. Cetto wineries, seen on each side of the road. Here also is the northern access to the Valle de Guadalupe, and Baja's wine country.

A couple miles farther, the road branches, and you have to make a decision. Straight ahead lie the dual villages of Guadalupe and Francisco Zarco. Highway 3 however branches left, and you cross a bridge to the other side of the valley, where the road curves south for about fourteen miles before exiting Valle de Guadalupe at San Antonio de las Minas. From there you descend gradually to the Pacific Coast and the intersection with Highway 1. The fascinating story of Valle de Guadalupe, its people and its wineries is detailed in the next chapter.

Chapter 3

Valle de Guadalupe

After the one and a half hour trip down Baja's stunning coastline described in the previous chapter, a looping overhead off-ramp announces the intersection with "Tecate 3." This lower status but reliably paved road is the entry point to Baja's fascinating Valle de Guadalupe. Six miles prior to reaching the port city of Ensenada, Highway 3 provides the only route for the lumbering double semi-trailers on their trek to Baja's other border crossing at Tecate. In a sense, here at Latitude 32.5 degrees North, and on Highway 3, is really where any Mexican wine odyssey begins. At this point, you are heading inland and northward towards arguably the most important wine producing area in all of Mexico.

Immediately appearing on both sides of the road are dozens of *maquiladoras*. These are border industries that employ cheap Mexican labor to produce TVs, auto parts, and other necessities of American life. Past these buildings, the narrow two-lane road leads on through mesquite country toward the valley some fifteen miles further inland.

At this point the road begins to gradually rise, and a noticeable break in the hilly horizon appears ahead. The hills soon become part of a mountain range that blocks the view of what lies beyond. On each side of the road now are the occasional small ranchero, café, honey (*miele*) seller, and tiny shrine. The latter reminds you that these blind curves are still dangerous in the hands of the wrong driver.

At kilometer 97 (the kilometer signs count backward from Tecate) the road passes through a notch in the mountain and marks a descent into the broad fertile valley whose far end is known as the Valle de Guadalupe. At the valley floor near Km 95 is the tiny village of San Antonio de las Minas ("of the mines," probably copper). Recently, as described in the next chapter, this portion has been given its own valley appellation by its winemaking inhabitants: El Valle de San Antonio de las Minas. This stop in the road offers a friendly café and the first of the burgeoning number of wineries.

The valley itself sprawls northeastward from a southern start near San Antonio de las Minas. A broad floor, slightly squeezed in the middle, marks its presence and leads some 14 miles farther to a northern end approximately five miles beyond the village of Francisco Zarco. From there Highway 3 descends into a region of hotter, largely undeveloped farm-land and rugged hills. About thirty miles farther, the road enters Valle de las Palmas, an agricultural community that offers food, a Pemex station, and modest shopping opportu-nities. Another twelve meandering and hot miles through a few more vineyards (largely used in producing lesser bulk wine), ranches, and orchards, the road passes Rancho Tecate (on the left), a popular resort and spa. Soon after, the junction with Mexico Highway 2-D appears, followed by entrance into the friendly border community of Tecate, population of 50,000 and home of a Mexican beer by the same name. If you visit here, don't miss enjoying one of the delicious ice cream cones (safe to eat!) sold all around the town square. They offer for your discovery many wonderful flavors (e.g., Midnight Blue) never found in the U.S.

The Shape of Things

Located about fifteen miles from the Pacific Ocean, approximately 14 miles long and five miles at its widest, Valle de Guadalupe is shaped something like a fat-bottomed, lop-sided gourd with a weight problem. In overall area it is about two-thirds the size of Napa Valley. The jagged yet mesmerizing westerly mountains rise to rocky highs of 2600 to 3000 feet and join the broad valley floor at an average elevation of about 1100 feet. The Sierra Blanca range, some of whose peaks reach an impressive 3000 to 4000 feet, protects the northeastern side. The runoff from this range is the source of the Guadalupe River. Convergence of these rocky guardians at the north end of the Valley provides a sturdy protection against the hot desert conditions that lie beyond. At the same time they offer a steep-walled escape to Tecate that is followed by the continuation of Highway 3 out of the Valley. This is part of the Coastal Area of Baja, beginning at the California (U.S.) border and traveling south for about 170 miles, then moving inland from the Pacific Coast for about 35 miles. Here it joins the piedmont slope of the Sierra of Juarez which goes north-south and divides two climatic areas: the coastal to the west and the continental to the east. Geographically, the Valley is located at latitude 32.5 degrees north, just within the Northern Hemisphere's mid-latitude belt of wine-producing countries that circles the globe between the 30th and 50th parallels.

Map of the Valle de Guadalupe. Larger enclosed area shows locations of current commercial wineries. The smaller enclosed area indicates the sub-viticultural region named San Antonio de las Minas. (Courtesy: Global Graphics)

This would all be quite unremarkable if it were not for three factors that profoundly affect the Valley's usefulness as a source of quality wine grapes. First and foremost is the prominent notch in the mountain range through which most traffic enters the valley from the southwest end, for this offers a portal to a regular early-evening visitor of a different nature. It is this flow of misty Pacific marine air and the Valley's largely east-west orientation that dramatically cools the valley floor and brings out the jackets of those who chose to stay for a summer's evening concert. Even more importantly, this cool air offers the ripening grapes a needed respite from the summer's daily heat. Secondly, the water table is a mere six feet underground, and this permits drip irrigation and dry farming throughout most of the Valley floor.

View of the "notch" near the summit while traveling northwest on Highway 3, just prior to descending into the southern end of the Valley.

Last among these remarkable features of nature, the Guadalupe River's passage through the valley from northeast to south-west offers a moderating influence on the day and night temperature extremes. The resulting Mediterranean-like cli-mate displays average temperatures ranging from 46ºF to

70ºF, with absolute minimums and maximums recorded as 25ºF and 106ºF. Average relative humidity is usually 70-75% with almost frost-free springs, which minimizes the chance for mold production. During the November to March rainy season, the annual average precipitation is about ten inches. Do not assume, however, that this means that the Guadalupe River is simply a charming addition to the landscape. Although a gently flowing stream most of the time, in harsher winters its power is mighty, and at least once in recent history its waters have wiped out dwellings and forced relocation of village Francisco Zarco's inhabitants to higher ground. From the southwest end of the valley, two successive right-angle turns lead the Rio Guadalupe back northward out of the

Photo taken in 1935 of a vineyard planted in 1918 near what is now the village of Francisco Zarco. Olive trees are in the foreground and a box for the harvest. The Guadalupe River appears in the background. (Courtesy: C. Magoni)

Valley. From there it flows downward into a neighboring steep-walled valley occupied by the village of La Misión, before reaching its Pacific terminus.

Soil types vary, with alluvial, sandy soils deposited over eons of time onto the Valley's flat floor. The hillsides exhibit decomposed granite, and the western area tends toward loam or sandy-loam soil. The reddish appearance suggests a significant iron content in the soil that has been swept down through the numerous alluvial fans that descend from the surrounding mountains. All the soils are reported to have excellent drainage that encourages good root development.

Of the Valley's approximately twenty-five square miles of smooth floor (16,000 acres), currently 7,000 acres, or almost 44 percent, are committed to vineyards, with most oriented either east/west or north/south. So far there has been no evidence of phylloxera infestation, caused by a root louse that weakens and eventually kills the vine; no current cure is known other than replanting on resistant rootstock. However, some vines nearest the river have shown signs of oidium fungus (powdery mildew), a bothersome but treatable infestation.

Traces of a milder form of Pierce's Disease have also appeared in some vines planted in the sandy soil near the riverbed, caused by a bacterium spread by winged insects called the blue-green sharpshooter. These insects, being much smaller than their ugly relative, the glassy-winged sharpshooter, feed only on the leaves. Although the latter is not a serious threat yet in the Valley, with currently no effective treatment the glassy-winged version has wreaked havoc in California's Temecula wine region, and has winemakers further north worried also. Once infected, the vine dies within one to four years. Active research on prevention and cure is underway at the University of California, sponsored by California's Department of Food and Agriculture, and Temecula's vineyards are making an encouraging comeback.

Origins

Long before commercial winemakers settled in the Valley, evidence supports the existence of local Indians inhabiting the area. They gathered seeds, pine nuts, fruits, acorns, and root vegetables, and hunted in a semi-nomadic system. Semi-permanent small settlements called "rancherías," supported as many as two hundred people, and consisted of several crude huts. These huts usually were made by inserting flexible willow branches into the ground in two parallel rows, bending the tops over and piling other brush on top of the tied branches and at one end. Smaller huts were conical, with the branches coming together in a pointed roof.

Modern vineyards and rocky mountains coexist in the Valle de Guadalupe (Courtesy: F. Favela)

In the 1600's these hunter-gatherers roamed the Baja peninsula and were part of almost 50,000 indigenous people that populated the area. This is not to say that they were all friendly neighbors, or that communication was easy or encouraged among the numerous tribes. In fact, with a population density of less than one person per square mile it was often easy for the rancherías to ignore each other. Today, it is generally accepted that there were three major peninsular linguistic groups, with tribes contributing further dialect diversification. As early as 1935, Peveril Meigs, in his book "The Dominican Mission Frontier of Lower California" (1935), noted "Indians of the entire upper half of the Baja peninsula seemed to share a common linguistic stock known as 'Yuman'." It is said that the Akwa'ola, possible descendents of the earlier Ñakipas or Yakakwatl tribes, were linguistically associated with those known as the Pai-Pai ("Clever People"). Other peoples were known as Kumiai or Kamia or Ipai, Cucapá and Kiliwa. By the time missionaries began to occupy the region however, inhabitants of adjacent rancherías were often speaking mutually unintelligible dialects. The Spanish referred to them generically as the "*Diegueños del Sur*" (literally the "San Diego Southerners"), now known as Tipai.

This latter group settled mostly outside of the Valley, some fifty miles southeast, in a sprawling settlement now known as Héroes de la Independencia. This was approximately five miles north of what is now the southern portion of Highway 3, a twisting cross-Baja climb over the mountainous backbone between Ensenada and San Felipe. Dominican missionaries in 1797 founded nearby Santa Catarina (now Ejido Rincon Santa Catarina, but known then by the indigenous name, "*Xac Tojol*"). In 1840 the local tribes of Pai-Pai, Kumiai, Kiliwa and Cucapá revolted and destroyed it.

The Kumiai however had settled in several locations within the municipalities ("counties") of Tecate and Ensenada. The final and largest community still exists within the Valley, ten miles to the north of Ejido El Porvenir in the indigenous community of San Jose de la Zorra. *Ejido* literally means "common land," and typically was deeded by the Mexican government to a group of communal farmers for their exclu-sive use.

The population of la Zorra has dwindled to about eighty inhabitants, who seek to conserve elements of their culture, language, music, dance and basket weaving skills. These peoples referred to the area as *"Oja-Cuñurr"* or "Painted Cave" (*"Cueva Pintada"* in Spanish).

Missions

A more documented history begins in June of 1834 with the founding of Baja California's last mission, Misión de Nuestra Señora de Guadalupe del Norte by Father Felix Caballero, head of the Dominican Order's Baja missions. Significantly, this event occurred thirteen years after Mexico's declared independence in 1821 and 118 years before Baja California became a state of Mexico in 1952. The site of the mission (N32º05.51' W116º34.51') is about sixteen miles east of the mission San Miguel Arcángel de la Frontera ("of the Frontier") and was described by an Ensign Ildefonso Bernal in 1795 as being in the "Valle de San Marcos," and known locally as the "Valley of the Four Tongues."

Located in the village of Guadalupe, adjacent to its current neighbor Francisco Zarco (named after an admired Mexican journalist), the mission fathers began the cultivation of grains and planted a small fruit tree orchard. In addition, a vineyard was started, obviously to provide wine for the priest's religious services, as was the practice at all mission sites. These cultivated lands were irrigated with water brought to the mission from the east end of the Valley. A channel is thought to have achieved this by starting about one kilometer east of the current bridge that spans the Guadalupe River, north of what today is Francisco Zarco. The local indigenous population, some of whom participated in the mission's farming program, was estimated at about four hundred. By 1840 it is calculated that their herd of cattle numbered 4,915 head, the largest of all the Dominican missions.

Periodically the mission inhabitants repulsed attacks by members of small hostile rancherías who lived to the north and east of them. In 1837 however, the mission suffered extensive damage from a particularly powerful onslaught by four hundred Yuma Indians. That same year the Mexican government ordered the secularization of all missions and their conversion to parish churches. The mission lasted only three years longer and was destroyed in 1840 during a further incursion of hostile forces

Reconstruction of a Kumiai family dwelling at the Museo Comunitario del Valle de Guadalupe near Francisco Zarco.

(possibly inspired by similar uprisings that led to the destruc-tion of Mission Santa Catarina in the same year). Father Caballero was driven away, and the mission was permanently abandoned.

Russian Immigrants

Rancho de la Ex-misión de Guadalupe, as the area was appropriately renamed, had a series of politically important

Statues of the founders of two religious orders responsible for establishing many missions in Baja California. St. Francis of Assisi (Franciscan), at left and St. Dominic (Dominican), at right, flanking St. Augustine.

Remains of the Misión de Nuestra Señora de Guadalupe del Norte, located at the southern end of the village of Francisco Zarco.

owners until it was finally purchased from a bank on March 20,1906, by the Cooperative Society of the Russian Empress Colonizers of Baja California. The society represented about a hundred immigrant families who had left their city of Kars in Russia's Trans-Caucasus region (now part of Turkey). To do so required permission from Czar Nicolas II, and frankly he seemed glad to get rid of them. They differed with him regarding his rules for military service as well as for religious reasons, and were part of an independent sect known as the Molokans ("milk drink-ers"). Although not a fully documented term, some say that it originally was one of derision, applied to those who refused to obey the Russian Orthodox Church's abstinence rules and instead drank milk on fast days. In an interesting twist, the leaders were said to have then adopted the name for themselves because they were "drinkers of the spiritual milk of God." Others say that it was simply because, being dairy farmers, they made and ate a lot of cheese. Settling in the valley, they established a successful agricultural community, with other members seeking freedom of political and religious expression joining them later. Initially producers of wheat, later immigrants brought knowledge of grape-growing techniques and winemaking. Thus, the basis of a nascent viticulture industry formed within the Valley, albeit one that was still kept largely "within the family."

In 1937 the Molokans formed an "ejido" under the name "Guadalupe," a month later renamed "El Porvenir." This became the home community for most of the families, as it still remains today. Over the years the population grew to a maximum of nearly nine hundred people, by far the majority of them located in the Guadalupe Colony. In 1958 the Mexican government began construction of a new road from the valley south to Ensenada. Ironically this proved to be the beginning of the end for the Molokan Colony.

Mature vineyard in front of Bodegas de San Valentin, an early Molokan-owned winery and table grape producer in the Valle de Guadalupe. (Courtesy: C. Magoni)

A peasant activist from Baja named Braulio Maldinado owned about one hundred acres in the valley and held aspira-tions to be governor. When a number of laborers from Sonora, whom he had recruited to build the federal highway, sought farm employment in the United States they were refused entry. Seizing upon this as an opportunity to garner more votes, Maldinado promised them free land in the Guadalupe Valley if he were elected. Unfortunately, it was land owned by the Molokan Community.

In 1958 the Molokans were repeatedly invaded by large groups of unemployed workers who settled on the Community's fields and vineyards. Further, they claimed the land for themselves and in the name of the Mexican people. The irony of this was not lost on the fifty year-old Molokan Community, many of whose members were Mexican citizens themselves, having by now been born in the Valley, and others having married and adopted the names of their Mexican husbands.

Despite limited support from former president Cardenas, and eventual arrival some ten months later of federal troops to remove the first wave of squatters, trucks and buses continued to invade their fields and set up makeshift dwellings. The pacifist Molokans were reluctant to physically resist and their eventual legal efforts were too little and too late.

Although there is some dispute over what occurred next, most of the Molokan Community claim that Governor Maldonado expropriated 300 acres of their land to the squatters, who by then called themselves the Francisco Zarco group, after a young intellectual journalist of the early 1800's. Zarco wrote in support of reform laws and strongly opposed the reactionary government that eventually imprisoned him. With return of the republican government, he was elected to congress, but died poor at the age of forty. In October 1962, Baja governor Esquival recognized the claims of the squatters and rededicated the village of Guadalupe in the name of Francisco Zarco. By then many of the remaining Molokans had sold their land at depreciated prices and had emigrated to the United States.

Some members of the remaining group now grow wine grapes that they sell to Valley wineries. One Molokan-owned winery, Vinos Bibayoff, currently produces and sells several wines under its own label (see Bibayoff chapter).

It is well worth a stop on your way to the wineries to visit a small museum, "Museo Comunitario del Valle de Guadalupe" that was opened by the Mexican government in June 1991. At its dedication, Governor Ernesto Ruffo praised the "devotion and hard work the Molokans did for this nation," while omitting mention of the pain and sorrow the Molokans endured. The Museum maintains a fascinating collection of photos and artifacts about the valley, the Molokan community, its agrarian life, and its people who now number only about 100. In addition, the museum has collected historical and cultural information on the local Kumiai Indians. Directly across the street is a second museum and tiny restaurant named "Museo Comunitario del Valle de Guadalupe" (note the slight difference in name) begun by a different member of the community. These unique museums are located 1.5 miles west of the junction of Highway 3 and the gravel road into the villages of Francisco Zarco/Guadalupe. Watch carefully for them as you head toward Monte Xanic, Chateau Camou, Adobe Guadalupe or Vinos Bibayoff.

Wine Development

Although little else seems to be known about its origins, near the end of the nineteenth century, a vineyard is reported to have been planted in the middle-north part of the Valley on the road that led to a Rancho "Agua Escondido."

Although the Molokan community began planting vineyards in 1915, major valley wine development didn't begin until after 1930. With the strong support of General Abalardo Rodríguez, former president of Mexico and owner of the Bodegas de Santo Tomas, the first winery in Baja, significant plantings were begun in the Valley. Although originally located in the Valle de Santo Tomas, south of Ensenada, Rodríguez's entrepreneurial interests still led him to recognize the potential of viticulture and olive cultivation in the Valle de Guadalupe. The varieties grown at that time were predominately white: *Muscat, Mission, Palomino, White Malaga,* as well as the red varieties *Carignan* and *Zinfandel.* Of course at that time fortified wines dominated the market and table wines were still produced in small quantities.

In 1946, Esteban Ferro, general manager at Santo Tomas, introduced into the Valley several varieties obtained from Piedmont, Italy: *Nebbiolo, Barbera, Dolcetto, Grinolino, Freisa* and *Moscato di Canelli*. In 1956 the valley's first commercial winery, Formex Ibarra, was built near Francisco Zarco, producing wine marketed under the labels Terrasola and Urbinon. The winery closed in 1988.

Former President Lazarus Cardenas (3rd from left) with Molokan Russian leaders. (Courtesy: C. Magoni)

In 1960, the Angelo Cetto family, who owned a bottling facility in Tijuana, acquired 250 acres of vineyards in the Valley. In the sixties, *Valdepeñas* (*Tempranillo*), *Ruby Cabernet*, and *Colombard* were introduced. By 1968 the Cettos had purchased the El Escondido Ranch just south of Tecate with its 180 acres of dry-farmed *Zinfandel* vineyards. These had been planted in 1930 with cuttings imported from the Escondido area of California. For the next six years Angelo Cetto's eldest son, Luis Ferruccio, continued to acquire land in the Valley and plant it to vineyards.

By 1970 the greatest evolution in vineyard development in the Valley began with extensive plantings of high-quality varietals, including the reds: *Cabernet Sauvignon, Merlot, Petite Sirah*; and among the whites: *Chardonnay, Sauvignon Blanc* and *Chenin Blanc*. These became the basis for realizing quality viticulture in the Valley.

In 1972, Pedro Domecq built the first modern commercial winery, Vides del Guadalupe, at the northern end of the Valley, the huge producer of El Presidente Brandy and other distilled spirits. By 1973 it was shipping wines labeled as originating in the Valle de Calafia, a name that the winery gave to their portion of the Valle de Guadalupe. It was a clever move. The new designation distinguished Domecq from other Valley producers, as well as introduced a distinctive regional appellation, the ancient name of the legendary Amazon queen, from which "California" was derived. Further land acquisitions to the north and elsewhere permitted their production to expand dramatically. Soon the winery became known as Domecq Winery. Today it is called Casa Pedro Domecq, or simply "Domecq."

1974 saw the founding of Vinicola L.A. Cetto by Luis Agustín Cetto, by now sole owner of his family's growing wine business and located almost directly opposite Domecq on Highway 3. In 1990 further introduction of red varietals was made, including *Syrah, Sangiovese, Petite Verdot* and *Malbec*, as well as the new white varietal, *Viognier*. Systematic acquisition of vineyard property in other regions outside the Valley has brought their total holdings to about 2,500 acres. Today, Domecq and Cetto are the two largest producers of table wines in Mexico and account for nearly eighty percent of the 1.6 million cases of wine produced annually. Bodegas Santo Tomás is a distant third.

The Newcomers

During this period of development by Cetto and Domecq, and especially during the late 1980's, a flux of new wineries began to appear in the Valley. Similar in spirit to many boutique wineries founded in California during the same time period, these showed increased emphasis on small, limited production, and high-tech facilities run by professionally trained winemakers whose passion was to make ultra-premium quality wines. Almost from the beginning their well-funded programs began to bear fruit. Best known of these are Monte Xanic (1988) and Chateau Camou (1991). Having found specific microclimates to their liking just southwest of Francisco Zarco, they have built state-of-the-art wineries that hug the base of the dramatic, sharply rising and rocky line of hills that defines the northwest side of the western portion of the Valley. Here the valley floor rises a bit in elevation, and small canyons as well as the proximity of the mountainous and rocky hillside provide more sheltered, yet somewhat cooler conditions for their premium grapes.

Further south along the same gravel road Adobe Guadalupe (2001) and Vinos Bibayoff (1970s) display their wineries. Two more different facilities are hard to find in the Valley. Don and Tru Miller, the first U.S. Americans to have a wine connection in Valle de Guadalupe, own Adobe Guadalupe. Perhaps as a sign of the times, they began by building a Mediterranean-styled guest inn near El Porvenir, a few miles beyond Chateau Camou. The planting of a vineyard of premium varietals and the adjacent construction of a small winery and horse stables soon followed. Just southwest of Adobe Guadalupe is still another new small winery named Rincon de Guadalupe.

David Bibayoff Dalgoff today owns Vinos Bibayoff. He is the grandson of Alexi M. Dalgoff who originally received permission to make wine on this property from the governor of Baja in the early 70's. It is located approximately six miles along the gravel road beyond Francisco Zarco at Rancho Toros Pintos. Here the Valley broadens into a sprawling ranchland area. The winery harvests many of its grapes from mature vineyards planted many years ago. In a direct way Bibayoff has evolved from the grape-growing tradition of the Molokan Russians, who arguably could be credited with starting the commercial side of all this.

Meanwhile, scattered alongside Highway 3 on the south-easterly side of the valley floor, several other wineries have established themselves,. Don Raúl Borquez started Bodegas de San Antonio in 1986. Located in San Antonio de las Minas (technically in a little valley of its own at the west end of Valle de Guadalupe), it was purchased recently by Bodegas Santo Tomás and renamed Rancho Nova de Bodegas de Santo Tomás. It will be run as a separate entity, producing its own line of premium wines. Nearby is Casa de Piedra, whose first vintage was vinified in 1997 by Hugo D'Agosta, former winemaker at Santo Tomás. Mogor-Badan, (Km 86.5) was started in 1987 on Rancho El Mogor, where Frenchman Henri Badan and his young wife had settled in 1948 to grow carob trees. Not surprisingly, engineer, owner and winemaker Antonio Badan specializes in Bordeaux and Swiss varietals. In 1991 Engineer Eduardo Liceaga Campos of Rancho El Paricutin (Km 93) began to graft over his vineyard of 10,000 table-grape vines to 60% *Merlot* and 40% *Cabernet Franc*. Naming his winery Viña de Liceaga, he produced his first vintage in 1993. The newest winery at this time is named Vinisterra S.A. de C.V., and has located in a converted house in San Antonio de las Minas, while it builds its new winery.

The Valley now boasts nearly 7,000 acres planted to all the premium wine varietals. In addition, more than 1,500 workers labor in the noble task of carefully tending these grapes and ensuring every year their successful transformation into the many varieties of wine now being produced in the Valle de Guadalupe.

Vides del Guadalupe, founded in 1972 by Pedro Domecq, now known as Casa Pedro Domecq.

Vinicola L.A. Cetto, founded in 1974. Together with Pedro Domecq, produces nearly eighty percent of wine made in Mexico.

Chapter 4

The Other Valleys

Valle de Santo Tomás

Upon leaving Ensenada, Highway 1, a four-lane undivided but well-paved road, heads south. After passing several commercial districts, the Ensenada Airport, and a military camp, the area on either side becomes increasingly agricultural. Gradually the coast disappears behind a growing chain of steep hills that prevent any further view of the Pacific. Soon the road passes through a broad agricultural flatland filled with olive trees, chili peppers, and other warm weather vegetable crops. About eleven miles out of Ensenada it enters Maneadero, the bustling agricultural market center for the area, with a population of about 55,000. Here also is the junction with BCN 23 that leads to Punta Banda, a rocky peninsula that terminates at its tip with the spectacular natural sea spout known as La Bufadora. Although touristy, the fifteen-mile drive offers incredible views of the Pacific and of Bahía de Todos Santos ("Bay of All Saints"), the graceful harbor that protects Ensenada from the harshest of winter storms, and is well worth the drive.

Quickly moving out of the open countryside, the road narrows significantly, just in time to climb and twist along the mountainous divide that precedes an inevitable drop into the Valle de Santo Tomás. With this increase in elevation, visitors move dramatically from tilled soil to chaparral-covered slopes and sense a distinct absence of coastal breeze. Finally, now 30 miles south of Ensenada, the road spirals down into the largely vineyard-covered Santo Tomás Valley, a protected oblong bowl approximately six miles long and about one and one-half miles at its widest. Unmistakably settling below on the left, like a half-buried Aztec temple, is the namesake winery's new low-slung gravity-flow facility. In the distance, on the other side of the valley floor, is a cluster of small buildings. This is the tiny village of Santo Tomás, containing a Pemex station,

The Valle de Santo Tomás, viewed from its northern entrance. In the near foreground is the new gravity-flow winery of Bodegas de Santo Tomás. The valley is situated east-west, with its terminus at the Pacific Ocean to the right, out of view. The final site of the Misión de Santo Tomás is situated on the far side of the Valley, near the grove of trees in the distance. On Highway 1, several trucks climb towards the viewer. Highway 1 continues south across the valley to its next destination, the Valle de San Vicente.

trailer park, general store, and the final remains of the Mission of Santo Tomás de Aquino. To the right the valley gradually narrows, and except in draught years, becomes a marshy canyon whose stream meanders for about twelve miles to its terminus in a small lagoon that empties into the Pacific Ocean.

In sharp contrast to the well-manicured vineyards that carpet portions of the valley floor today were the conditions encountered by the Dominican missionaries when they first entered the valley in 1785 (then known as Valle de San Solano). The writer Peveril Meigs, in his book *The Dominican Mission Frontier of Lower California (1935)*, describes their original preferred 1785 site as a side canyon with a source "of water flowing from a marsh, enough good land for the planting of more than ten *fanegas* (26 bushels) of *maize* (corn), a good place for building houses, and an abundance of willows, sycamores, and live oaks—'enough for three missions.' Pasture abounded in the main valley. Although favored by the initial group of missionary visitors, the then Governor Fages rejected the site (too narrow, flood vulnerable, lack of sunlight). They compromised, and favored instead one at the lower end of the Valle de San Solano.

Thus vicar Juan Crisóstomo Gómez and José Loriente finally founded the Dominican's fifth mission on April 24, 1791, and named it Mission Santo Tomás de Aquino. F. C. Negrete, in 1853, said that it was settled at a place called *Copaitl coajocuc* (crooked sycamore) "on the skirt of the hills on the north of the arroyo, about a league (3 mi.) to the west of where it is today (1853)." Due to the close proximity to a marsh that provided an abundant and constant source of mosquitoes, the original site soon proved to be a poor choice. By the end of the first year, only three men and two women remained healthy. In 1794 they moved to a final site at the village of Santo

Tomás where the mission remained until 1849, when it was the last to be abandoned. Following the Dominicans' departure it was used for a while as a frontier military garrison.

As true today as when Meigs described it during his visit in 1929, "The alluvial valley floor, a veritable plain, stretches east and west for ten miles, with an average width of about a mile. Mountain walls, mostly of resistant intrusives and metamorphics, rise in a continuous barrier along the sides to elevations of from 500 to 2000 feet above the floor. Toward the west the sides of the valley gradually converge into the outlet, Santo Tomás Cañon, a hundred yards wide, winding twelve miles westward to the sea, and dropping three hundred feet." He also noted, "it has the customary foggy desert climate of the northwestern part of the Peninsula" with nocturnal "high fog" drifting in on "the usual northwest wind." The fog lasted no later than 9 a.m. of the next morning, when "the clearing began in the east, the eastern edge of the fog retreating seaward by evaporation."

Still, daytime temperatures can rise above 80 degrees Fahrenheit, with temperatures at night capable of falling well below 60 degrees, favorable viticultural conditions for premium wine grape production. Today, where the land hasn't been turned over to vineyards, you can see grass and low shrubs, with the occasional clump of willow, cottonwood and elder trees. These signal the presence of numerous streams that enter the valley and form the moist land that characterizes portions of the valley floor, especially toward the west end. Live oaks grow in the drier sections on the southwest side where the valley wall begins to rise.

During its half century of existence as a mission, the clergy realized that the valley was a favorable place to plant and grow the *Mission* grapes that the founders had brought with them (All

The recently completed winery of Bodegas de Santo Tomás. Note the ramp at left that enables trucks to haul harvested grapes, dumping them directly into the crusher/destemmer units. The juice then flows by gravity to the next levels for fermentation, aging and barrel storage.

indications point to irrigation, not dry farming as having been the usual practice.). Although the original mission inhabit, ants appear to have irrigated only sixty-five acres, records indicate that more than two hundred acres were eventually cultivated by irrigation, including some 2000-5000 grape, vines. This expansion suggests that they produced a consider, able amount of wine during that time. Later efforts, however, seem to have included lower-yielding dry-farming techniques as well. In 1935, Meigs noted that for various purposes the inhabitants were dry-farming about seven hundred fifty acres of land (today, all the Santo Tomás Winery vineyards are either drip irrigated or dry-farmed).

When the federal government nationalized all church property in 1857, the State claimed ownership of the Valle de Santo Tomás. Largely for their own consumption, the seven or eight families living in the village at that time still used the stream at the mouth of the valley to support a few orchards, vineyards and corn patches. Don Loreto Amador, a resident of

Santo Tomás, then acquired the former mission's vineyards and used them in commercial production of wine on a ranch known as Rancho de los Dolores. This mildly successful operation lasted for 31 years until Don Francisco de Andonegui and Don Miguel Ormart, two enterprising European busi‚ nessmen more recently from Ensenada, bought it in 1888. They founded Bodegas de Santo Tomás and began to sell and distribute the wines in bulk directly to the various small towns of the region. This established the winery as the second oldest in Mexico and the oldest in Baja California.

A view southwest across the Valle de Santo Tomás. In the back‚ ground, there is an oak grove where the valley floor remains dry. At right, the valley becomes marshland, terminating at the Pacific Ocean.

In 1930 General Abelardo Rodríguez, governor of Baja California, purchased eight hectares of vines planted to *Mission* and *Roso del Perú* grapes and two thousand hectares of bare land from Andonegui for $28,000. Earlier, as Secretary of Indus‚ try and Commerce, Rodriguez appointed Esteban Ferro, a young Italian enotechnologist, to study the feasibility of the tiny vitivinicultural industry. A favorable report led Rodriguez to hire Ferro to operate his newly acquired winery.

Misión de Santo Tomás in 1926 at its final site near the southern exit from the Valley. The remains are located across from a Pemex station, within a small amusement park. (Courtesy: Engelhardt)

In 1931 Ferro moved the winery to downtown Ensenada and commenced to install new equipment imported from Italy and Germany. The first wines were produced in 1934 from grapes grown in the valleys of Santo Tomás and Redondo. Ferro imported Italian varieties such as *Barbera, Nebbiolo* and *Dolcetto* from his native Piedmont and acquired French varieties from Wente Brothers in California. The early sixty's saw Santo Tomás begin to modernize further their valley production under the direction of their newly hired Technical Director Dimitri Tschelischeff. He replaced many of their older vineyard varieties (*Mission, Colombard, Valdepeñas* [*Tempranillo*], *Grenache,* and *Barbera*) with *Cabernet, Pinot Noir, Riesling, Chenin Blanc* and *Chardonnay.* In 1995 work began on a state-of-the-art gravity-flow winery in Valle de Santo Tomás; currently it is in operation. Santo Tomás plans to make it their primary

View to the north from the top of the Santo Tomás Winery. Work buildings and remains of the original winery are located within the grove of trees.

View of the lowest level of the winery where new wines are stored in barrels for aging.

Ruins of Misión de San Vicente Ferrer, currently under restora-
tion.

production plant for red wine, since they grow many of their
grapes in the Santo Tomás and nearby San Vicente valleys.
Sparkling wine and bottling, however, are limited to their
Ensenada facility.

Valle de San Vicente

Passing south across the east end of Valle de Santo Tomás,
Hwy 1 continues approximately 23 miles further through
steep granitic hills and grassy valleys. At this point it enters the
old Valle de San Vicente, with the ruins of Mission San
Vicente Ferrer located at the end of a rough half-mile dirt road
leading to the right, off Hwy 1. Founded in 1780 at a site then
known variously as Santa Rosalía and Santa Isabel, the
Dominicans chose wisely.

At the northern edge of a mountain-rimmed alluvial plain
that geographer Meigs in 1929 named the "San Vicente
Basin," the San Vicente River enters from the east and has
carved out a narrow east-west canyon across the plain. At its

westernmost end lies the valley that once bore the same name; beyond this narrow valley, the river cuts through the tough western mountains before spilling into the Pacific. A sandy non-cultivatable arroyo runs through the valley to the sea, while largely granitic and hard rock walls rise on each side. Located near the western edge of the basin, the missionaries chose this valley as their site. At its northeast end they built their mission upon a gently sloping platform some ten feet above the arroyo and its potentially flooding waters.

This site, founded north of the second mission (Santo Domingo) in the "Five Mission Plan" of the Dominicans, furthered their goal to establish a chain of missionary command along the Baja peninsula. These were truly frontier missions and, as such, their sites had to provide some degree of security. In addition, they served as a source of native converts, labor and agricultural growth for the eventual conquest of the region. Diary accounts by the widely roaming Fray Juan Crespi (1769-1774) described the area prior to settlement as 'a large plain, with green grass, a marsh, plenty of water in the arroyo, and arable land: a good site for a mission.' This was very significant, and contrasted sharply with Santo Domingo, a less than an ideal mission, plagued by lack of military support and frequent native desertions. Also, time and effort were further expended by Santo Domingo's removal to a second site. Mission San Vicente Ferrer, on the other hand, was one of the very few which the Dominicans did not relocate.

Meigs noted in his 1937 account "strategically, San Vicente was better adapted as the chief stronghold of the Frontera than any other mission center. It was centrally situated in relation to the five "Pacific Missions," yet at the same time it lay opposite the part of the frontier most exposed to Indian attacks. The dangerous direction was the east, where, from San Pedro Martir north, there were numbers of wild Indians against whom protection was more than once necessary. The Arroyo of San Vicente led from the heart of this unsubdued country to San Vicente, providing a natural avenue for Indian attacks...After the foundation of Santa Catalina (seventeen years after San Vicente) San Vicente continued to be important as the base of support for this exposed mission." Although the military numbered only two or three dozen men, they apparently were hardy and loyal and kept the area relatively safe. Despite the epidemics that devastated the missions in 1782 and 1805, the native mission population reached a maximum of 317 in 1787. In the former site, they buried 27 percent of the population.

Both north and west of the mission, as well as south of the arroyo, are fertile lands that were cultivated. Beyond are suitable grazing and farming land that is still used today. However, unlike the Guadalupe and Santo Tomás Valleys, the San Vicente River meanders west through a barrier of mountains that prevents access to the moderating coastal breeze and its favorable inland influence on viticulture. Again, in contrast to the Valle de Santo Tomás, although ample water was available near the mission for irrigation, they chose to dry farm some of the land, and this practice continues today. The total cultivated area in mission days is believed to have numbered about 208 acres.

Thus, at about 650 feet above sea level, the designation "Valle de San Vicente" today describes much of the "Basin" into which the original valley/canyon was carved. About 0.7 mile beyond the mission ruins is the thriving town of San Vicente (population 6,000), which serves as the agricultural hub of the area. East of town, on the north slope, L.A. Cetto

A southeastern view towards the mountains defining the viticulture subregion of San Antonia de las Minas. Located within the southern end of the Valle de Guadalupé.

has 124 acres of vines, as well as an additional 124 acres west of town. Some seven miles further south, at Rancho Llano Colorado is an 860-acre site that supplies grapes to a number of wineries. The fourth principal vineyard area is a source of grapes for Pedro Domecq and is near Cañon Calentura, some ten miles east of Llano Colorado. With somewhat milder winters and comparable summers, the region provides very rich, deep, reddish soil, heavier than that in the Valle de Guadalupe. Grapes currently grown, primarily for L.A. Cetto and Santo Tomás, include *Chardonnay, Sauvignon Blanc, Barbera, Malbec, Nebbiolo, Petite Sirah* and *Tempranillo.*

Valle de San Antonio de las Minas

This small valley, previously considered a portion of the Valle de Guadalupe, offers a slightly different microclimate than its larger neighbor. It is located west of the town of the same name, shortly after coming down into the main valley. It lies closer to the Pacific Ocean than the rest of the valley and

experiences somewhat cooler growing conditions. Consequently, harvest is usually 2-3 weeks later than in other
regions. Currently the farmers grow *Cabernet Sauvignon*, *Merlot* and
Zinfandel there, and the grapes usually produce very concentrated wines.

Valle de Tecate

This very small valley, located right at the U.S./Mexico
border, is approximately 25 miles from the Pacific Ocean. A
175-acre vineyard of *Zinfandel*, planted in 1930, is dry farmed
by L.A. Cetto for use in their wines. It is on its own rootstock;
and the warmer microclimate, plus maturity of the vines,
yields a moderate crop of "old vines" style grapes of this
varietal.

Winery Organization

Part 2 is divided into two sections: Urban and Valley Wineries. Within each section the wineries are listed in order of their founding. Thus, you will find Baja California's oldest winery, Bodegas de Santo Tomás, appearing first among Ensenada's two urban wineries, and Pedro Domecq, the oldest Guadalupe Valley winery, starting the current commercial list of valley occupants. Although it is unlikely that more wineries will settle in downtown Ensenada (advantage: roughly equidistant from the two major valleys; disadvantage: grapes have to be shipped to the winery for processing, often during hot weather), a half-dozen Guadalupe winemakers are just over the horizon and on the verge of "going commercial."

Each winery's chapter opens with an "Essentials" section that provides the necessary information for finding and contacting the winery, plus other relevant data such as tasting room hours (when there are any), owner's and wine maker's names, production figures, etc. Although this is the most current information available at publication, please remember that this is still an emerging and developing region with informal procedures still in effect. If you are open to adventure, and don't mind a few delays or a return visit the next day, then follow your own tour instincts. If you want to be sure that a winery will be open when you arrive, then phoning ahead might be a good idea.

The sections on winery history, winemaker notes and vineyard/fermentation techniques should provide sufficient background to prepare the most ardent wine enthusiast. The wine notes have been carefully prepared to help you select specific wines to taste and to know what you can expect from each. In the smaller wineries you often will have the opportunity to actually meet the owner or wine maker (sometime this is the same person) and ask them questions about their wines. Having read something about them before you arrive should make you visit more enjoyable. All of them have invested much time and labor in making their product and will be pleased to respond to thoughtful questions. In the larger tasting rooms the opportunity for questions and comments is more limited, especially if you are competing with an enthusiastic crowd of tasters for the attention of the pourer(s). If this situation arises, then simply enjoy and share your impressions with your friends.

Part 2
The Wineries

Wine Awards

Wineries seek recognition for their wines in various ways, and each way lends a degree of credibility to the claim that their wines are worthy of respect. No single award is going to prove that a wine is "best," or will a collection of medals make one wine superior to another. Part of the problem lies in the sad fact that not all wines are entered in a single competition. Further, not all judges are equally skilled or trained to discern the qualities or flaws that make a wine noteworthy in a given event. In fact, a panel of perfectly competent judges may simply disagree as to what makes a wine a "winner"

Nevertheless, such awards continue to be sought after by wineries and when so recognized, they are announced with considerable pride. Included among such events is the annual wine competition that precedes the Vendimia (see Part 4) held in Ensenada in August. From personal experience, I can attest that the rules governing this international judging are very rigorous, although few California vintners choose to enter their wines.

Since many wine enthusiasts pay attention to these awards, I have included them in my wine comments when known.

Chapter 5

Ensenada's Urban Wineries

Avenida Miramar, several blocks north of Ensenada's harbor. On the corner is La Embotelladora Vieja, one of the city's excellent restaurants which serves many Baja wines. Adjacent is the tasting room of Bodegas de Santo Tomás.

Bodegas de Santo Tomás

Ensenada headquarters of Bodegas de Santo Tomás. The large adobe corner structure was originally the Ensenada jail.

The Essentials

Address: 666 Calle Miramar, Ensenada

Telephone: 646-178-3333

Fax: 646-178-3621

Email: bstwines@telnor.net

Web Page: www.santotomas.com

Established: 1888

Owners: Elías Pando, S.A. de C.V.

Winemaker: Octavio Gioia

Tasting Room: Daily, Tours 11 am, 1 & 3 pm, tour charge

Current Production: 85,000 cases

Capacity: 100,000 cases

Vineyard Size: 865 acres (350 Ha) property, 420 acres (170 Ha) in vines

Grape Varieties

Red: Cabernet Sauvignon, Merlot, Barbera, Cabernet Franc, Tempranillo, Grenache, Syrah

White: Chardonnay, Chenin Blanc, Sauvignon Blanc, Colombard, Riesling, Viognier

Winery History

The origin of Santo Tomás is inextricably tied to the Spanish mission movement in Mexico. Wherever a new mission was established in the New World, vineyards were planted and sacramental wine was made. Eventually, Spain's intent to Christianize the native populations led the missionaries with their cuttings as far west as Baja California. Here they began to build a series of missions along what are now the Baja and California coasts. By the time they decided to found a mission just south of Ensenada, the Dominican order was in charge. In 1791 they named it the Mission of Saint Tomas Aquinas, located in what is today the Valle de Santo Tomás (see "Other Valleys" chapter).

The Valle turned out to be a very favorable location for both the mission and sacramental wine production. But in 1857, after 66 years of the mission's existence, the Mexican government expropriated all church property and the land was sold off. Don Loreto Amador, a resident of the village of Santo Tomás, then acquired the former mission's vineyards and used them in commercial production of wine on a ranch known as Rancho de los Dolores. This operation lasted for 31 years until Don Francisco de Andonegui and Don Miguel Ormart, two Ensenada businessmen, bought it in 1888. They founded Bodegas de Santo Tomás and began to sell and distribute the wines in bulk directly to the various small towns of the region.

This established the winery as the second oldest in Mexico and the oldest in Baja California.

In 1929 they moved their operations to downtown Ensenada. As noted earlier in the chapter on "Other Valleys," General Abelardo Rodriguez, then governor of Baja California, purchased eight hectares of vines planted to Mission and Roso del Perú grapes and two thousand hectares of bare land from Andonegui in 1930 for $28,000. Earlier, as Secretary of Industry and Commerce, Rodriguez had appointed Esteban Ferro, a young Italian enotechnologist, to study the feasibility of the emerging vitivinicultural industry. A favorable report led Rodriguez to hire Ferro to operate his newly acquired winery.

In 1931 Ferro moved the winery to its current Ensenada site and commenced to install new equipment imported from Italy and Germany. The first wines were produced in 1934 from grapes grown in the valleys of Santo Tomás and Redondo. Ferro also imported cuttings of Italian varieties, such as *Barbera, Nebbiolo* and *Dolcetto,* from his native Piedmont. Sadly the workers hired to plant them in the nursery hopelessly mixed them together and many of the planted vineyards became Italian "field blends," making rather good Italian-like wine blends that were labeled as "Barbera." Around that time Ferro also acquired cuttings of some French varieties from Wente Brothers in Northern California. By 1937 Ferro was bringing in grapes harvested in Southern California to meet their demand for wine. During the Second World War, bottles, lead capsules, and labels were in short supply in Mexico, but Santo Tomás was able to import them from the United States. With the departure of Esteban Ferro, changes in management, and throughout the decade from 1952 to 1962, Santo Tomas nonvintage wines suffered a decline in quality and image that unfortunately became identified with Mexican wines in general.

The early sixty's saw Santo Tomás begin to modernize their valley production under the direction of their newly hired (1962) Technical Director Dimitri Tschelischeff, son of legendary Napa winemaker Andre Tschelischeff. According to Tchelistcheff, around 1956 Fernando Rodriguez, son of General Rodriguez, imported the varieties *Grenache*, *Burger*, and *Muscat of Alexandria*, and did fairly extensive plantings of these grapes in Guadalupe Valley. Dimitri states, "These grapes were greatly appreciated at the winery in Ensenada over the *Misión* and insipid *Palomino* varieties." In January of 1963 Tchelistcheff imported 200,000 cuttings from California: 150 thousand of *Valdepeñas* (*Tempranillo*) and 25 thousand of *Colombard* from E & J Gallo Winery where he had worked previously, and 25 thousand of *Chenin Blanc* from Beaulieu Vineyards where his father was Winemaker. Dimitri notes that these cuttings were planted in a nursery in the Valle de la Calentura (San Vicente), and later many were planted for Bodegas de Santo Tomás in San Vicente Valley. Dimitri says "to my knowledge this was the first and perhaps the only importation of these varieties to Baja. Later on, while on a trip to Spain I noticed that the variety we called *Valdepeñas* was identical to the *Tempranillo* of the Rioja and was grown in the Valdepeñas region as well." Dimitri recalls that the field blends of Italian red grapes planted in the Santo Tomás, San Vicente and Guadalupe Valleys, some of which remain today, were referred to as "Italian Varieties." Since the blend did contain "a good percentage" of *Barbera*, when he received the harvest from these blocks he simply called them *Barbera* on the winery records, as he had a liking of that variety from his work at E & J Gallo Winery. In fact, Dimitri says, "We came out with a Cosecha

1962 *Barbera* and kept it up through the years until today. Unfortunately my blocks of "Italian Varieties" planted by Esteban Ferro "pooped out" by 1971 and were pulled out. This was due to a severe attack by nematodes. Seeing this happening several years previously, I brought in pure *Barbera* from E & J Gallo Winery and grafted it on 1613 rootstock (very resistant to nematodes). This was done in both Santo Tomás Valley and Rancho Santa Isabel at San Vicente." In the early seventies Tchelistcheff imported *Cabernet Sauvignon* from France, and *Chardonnay* and *Pinot Noir* from Beaulieu Vineyard in Napa. He reports that the *Pinot Noir* surprisingly "did quite well in quality," but the management discouraged its use since it was a low producer and it was eventually pulled out. Some of the *Chardonnay* remains in Santa Isabel and in San Antonio de las Minos (in Guadalupe Valley). In addition to his efforts to raise the quality of Baja's wines, Dimitri is also credited with successfully producing one of the first commercial sparkling wines in Baja. After his departure at the end of 1976, Santo Tomás added more French and German varieties, including *Ruby Cabernet, Sauvignon Blanc, Cabernet Franc, Merlot, Pinot Noir, Riesling,* and *Chardonnay.*

In 1995 work began on a state-of-the-art gravity-flow winery in Valle de Santo Tomás. The facility is currently in operation, and Santo Tomás plans to make it their primary production plant. With many of their grapes grown in the Santo Tomás and nearby San Vicente valleys, they now can keep the time between harvest and crusher to a minimum. Sparkling wine and bottling will be limited to their Ensenada facility. In 1996, enologists Willy Joslin of Wente in Livermore, California, and Hugo D'Acosta of Santo Tomás joined forces to produce the first commercial wine made from California and Baja grapes. It was appropriately named *Duetto*. The Elias

Pando Corporation, a Mexican consortium that primarily produces canned goods, acquired the winery in 1962 and is their current owner.

Winemaker Notes

Consultant Enrique Ferro states that "Winemaking at Santo Tomás remains very traditional, yet modern techniques are being applied to those aspects of the program that can lead to improved quality and excellence in the final product and customer satisfaction. Some traditional practices are still done by hand, including weed management, leaf pulling and skirting, as well as grape harvesting. New trellising methods have been installed.

Many of the winery techniques at Santo Tomás also remain traditional, yet effective. Starting with the oak tanks and barrels, for over forty years Santo Tomás has employed a trained barrel maker to build them on site. Modern stainless steel, temperature-controlled fermenters are used to make the white wines, and 100% gravity flow methods are practiced at our new winery in the Santo Tomás Valley. Tradition continues however, even to the hand wrapping of each premium bottle in fine tissue paper before packing."

Vineyard and Fermentation Techniques

According to consultant Enrique Ferro, wines are planted at a density of 8 feet by 6 feet, the average age of the vines is 25 years, and the average yield is 8 Tons/ha (3.2T/acre). The trellis system used for many years consisted of 2 single catch wires, known as the California Sprawl, used extensively elsewhere for growing table grapes. This method, however, has fallen out of favor among international viticulturists because it demands heavy and costly canopy management for tip trimming (skirting) and leaf pulling in order to produce high quality wine grapes. New plantings of *Barbera, Syrah* and *Viognier,* were recently trellised with the VSP (vertical shoot positioning or vertical curtain) method, where two pairs of movable wires pull up the shoots as they elongate. This is the most popular and widely applied trellis system in Europe, especially for low to medium fertility soils, and the only one for mid-high densities such as those practised at BST. The sandy soils are host to several pathogenic nematodes and they are controlled biologically with a product made of parasitoid fungi.

White and rosé wines are cold stabilized in the old chilling room that was constructed by Esteban Ferro over 65 years ago, using thick walls of corks for insulation material. Native strains of bacteria are allowed to inoculate the wines for malolactic fermentation, rather than using commercial cultures. Small lots of red grapes from selected vineyard sites are fermented in open barrels with the cap of grape skins punched down by hand. Adding egg whites to the fermented product, followed by settling in large tanks, completes the clarification and fining of the wines. Tanks and barrels are topped each week year round to insure against air oxidation. Once a tank or barrel is emptied its interior is effectively sterilized with high temperature steam before it is reused.

The Wines

Duetto: By far their highest profile item (check the distinctive label) as well as their most pricey, *Duetto* is evolving under duel parentage into a very stylish wine. Produced jointly with grapes from Santo Tomás and Wente wineries (hence the name), it is also now a "duel-component" wine. Originally made from a blend of *Cabernet Sauvignon, Merlot* and *Cabernet Franc* grapes, it now is limited to *Cabernet Sauvignon* and *Merlot.* Proportions are still being tweaked somewhat, the current vintage ('99) blend being about 80/20. The first extensive release in the U.S. (1000 cases) was of the '97 vintage in February 2000. Garnet red in color, showing soft tannins, ripe fruit and hints of cocoa and toast, the wine finishes cleanly with lingering black fruit and light tobacco flavors. It has the potential to rest in the cellar for 2-5 years before that special meal. Serve with lightly sauced meats or stews.

Unico Gran Reserva: **Also a blend of** *Cabernet Sauvignon* **and** *Merlot,* **this is their "one winery" premium offering. Made of select grapes obtained from all three Baja valleys, it spends 18 months in small French oak barrels followed by one year in bottles prior to release. Ruby red color, the evident aromas are of dark fruit, toasted almonds and a hint of vanilla. Black stone fruit, soft mid-palate tannins, and moderate acidity present a balanced and structured aromatic flavor spectrum that finishes cleanly. Try with** *osso buco* **or mushrooms in puff pastry.**

Merlot: **Aged in French oak for six months and bottled for one year before release, this wine has wonderful deep red color. Its aroma will remind you of blueberries and cherries, its flavor of tart, dried cherries. Although its popularity seems to have stimulated a price increase, it remains a good value. Matches well with carne asada or baby back ribs.**

Barbera: **Aged for one year in oak barrels and given an additional year in bottle before release. First produced in 1962, this bright red wine displays typical** *Barbera* **aromas of cherries, leather and spices with a hint of oak. Followed by fruity flavors, a slight earthy sense and good varietal acidity, the mouth feel reveals slightly rustic, moderate mid-tannins.**

Multiple medal winner. Good with lasagna or a cassoulet. Drink now.

Tempranillo: A lighter-styled version of this varietal made from grapes grown in the Valle de San Vicente. Oakless, the wine goes directly to bottle for one year before release. The principal grape in Spanish Riojas, this pretty ruby wine shows pleasant berry aromas along with some leather and spices. Medium acidity and nice cherry fruit flavors are balanced with soft tannins and a clean finish. Multiple medal winner. Good with burgers or grilled pork.

Cabernet Sauvignon: 100 percent varietal, fermented in stainless steel with 20-30 days' maceration and aged one year in oak. Deep red color, complex aromas of red fruits blend with overtones of chocolate, coffee, leather and a hint of mint. Moderately firm tannins in a drying atmosphere challenge flavors of blackberry/cherry. Earlier vintages (first produced in 1973) are disappointingly dried out, although an '82 recently showed nice garnet color, aromas of dried stone fruit and rose petals, and still tasted of cherries and chocolate, but thin and astringent on a short finish. More recent winemakers have striven for a more friendly, fruitier style. Although a medal winner, other wines here seem to be more fun to drink. Serve with grilled meats or spiced duck breast.

Chardonnay: 100 percent varietal from grapes grown in the Valle de San Vicente. Fermented in stainless steel, followed by malolactic fermentation and *sur lies* in French oak barrels plus one year aging in bottle. Light straw color, aromatic mineral nose with vanilla, oak and butterscotch overtones. Bright tart-apple forward flavors show well in a smooth mouth filling structure with a short clean finish. Not real complex, but a pleasant drinker. Try with simple chicken dishes or pasta with mussels.

Sauvignon Blanc: 100 percent varietal from grapes grown in the Valle de San Vicente. Partial fermentation in stainless steel, finished *sur lies* in French oak barrels for about 5-6 months before bottling. Slight straw-green color, characteristic grassy-herbal, melony nose is accompanied by some oaky overtones. Spice and citrus flavors are balanced with good acidity and a clean finish. Not exactly the classic *Sauvignon Blanc* style, but try it; you may like it. Match with marinated shellfish or grilled vegetables.

Chenin Blanc: 100 percent varietal. Stainless steel fermentation and 5-6 month sur lies storage before bottling. Very light straw color, slight smoky nose with dominant banana and grapefruit aromas. Complex yet fresh floral/fruit and oak flavors with a long pleasant finish. Try with fruit salad or just for sipping on a hot afternoon.

Cavas Valmar

Winemaker and owner Fernando Martain of Cavas Valmar.

The Essentials

Address: 1950 Riveroll off Calle Ambar, Ensenada

Telephone: 646-178-6405

Fax: 646-178-6405

Email: valmar@telnor.net

Web Page: none

Established: 1983

Owners: Fernando Martain and Yolanda Valentin

Winemaker: Fernando Martain

Tasting Room: by appointment

Current Production: 2,500 cases/yr

Vineyard Size: Small, some grapes purchased

Grape Varieties

Red: Cabernet Sauvignon, Tempranillo, Grenache, Merlot

White: Chardonnay, Chenin Blanc

Winery History

Engineer Fernando Martain moved to Ensenada from Mexico City in the early 1980's to accept a job at Bodegas Santo

Tomás. While there, Martain met and married Yolanda Gayosso Valentin. Yolanda's grandfather, a French immigrant named Federico Valentin, enjoyed making wine from grapes grown at his rancho located to the north of downtown Ensenada. Once Don Federico learned of Martain's similar enthusiasm for winemaking, he encouraged the newly married couple along with his own two sons, Hector and Gontrán Valentin, to start making wine seriously. His advice to them was "to focus on making a little bit of good wine rather than a lot of average stuff." Thus in 1983 they founded Cavas Valmar, a small family run urban winery located on Don Federico's rancho. The name, of course, derived from the merging of the first three letters of the two family names, Valentin and Martain. At first, they made wine on an old parking lot at the rancho, with a small mill, a manual corking machine, a little basket press, and 20 American oak barrels. Their grapes were the old varietals of the region, including *Palomino, Ugni Blanc, Moscatel, Grenache*, and Italian varieties that had been introduced into the Guadalupe area. In 1985 Valmar introduced its first two commercial wines. As Fernando learned to master the complexities of growing grapes and making good wine, Valmar began by producing a modest 300 cases. Initial effort was focused on *Cabernet Sauvignon* and *Chenin Blanc*. However, the winery currently has expanded its production to 2,500 cases per year with the inclusion of *Tempranillo, Grenache* and *Chardonnay*. Other varietals may be added in the near future. More significantly perhaps is that Martain is selecting his grapes now from several different regions (in addition to the vineyard adjacent to the winery), to take advantage of the different microclimates available in this area, and to maximize the quality of his wines.

Winemaker Notes

"There are some very interesting valleys that haven't been exploited," says winemaker Martain. "One of these, in the San Vicente Valley, to the south of Ensenada, has vine stock more than forty years old. Its *Cabernet Sauvignon* grafts were implanted in 1983, and have yielded wines of great complexity and richness. Another vineyard with *Chenin Blanc* stock is located in the Valle de las Palmas to the northeast of Ensenada. Those vines have been in place more than twenty years and produce grapes noted for their bold fruity essences."

Vineyard and Fermentation Techniques

"The production of *Chenin blanc* begins in July when we visit the vineyards in order to monitor and revise the characteristics which we desire in the grape at the moment of harvest. Those include vigilant monitoring of sugar and acidity levels, selection of the parts of the vineyard that we like, and maintaining the best in cleanliness and foliage management, while avoidance of harm to the clusters. We begin the harvest in the early hours of the morning, and it's collected in plastic boxes with a maximum capacity of 10 kilograms, avoiding in this manner the loss of fruit character and degradation during its transport to the city of Ensenada. Fermentation is carried out at low temperature, approximately and on average at 12 degrees centigrade during two or three months, then clarified with a little gelatin, stabilized and bottled.

"Production of *Cabernet Sauvignon* begins in September with similar vineyard diligence and early morning harvest procedure. Fermentation for twelve days leads to the development of colors, flavors, and aromas that later lead to the characteristics of Valmar. When the fermentation has ended, the wine is placed in oak barrels until the completion of the secondary malolactic fermentation. For a final year the wine is transferred to other barrels to separate it from the sediment; the barrels are moved to a temperature and humidity controlled cave, where it remains a minimum of 12 months, before final clarification, filtration and bottling."

The Wines

Cabernet Sauvignon: 100% varietal, from grapes harvested in the Valleys of San Vicente, San Antonio de las Minas, and Guadalupe. Stainless steel fermented then transferred to French oak barrels for aging, it is a dark red color, with herbal, black cherry, coffee and vanilla aromas. Berry fruit, herbs and spice flavors are balanced against mild midforward tannins to provide a good structure with a dry, clean, somewhat short finish. Should gain in complexity and finesse with a year or two of bottle age. Good with grilled red meats, *poblanos rellenos*, and mature cheese.

Tempranillo: 100% varietal, from Valle de San Vicente. Stainless steel fermented then transferred to French oak barrels for aging. Dark ruby/violet color, with aromas of black cherry, vanilla and oak. Flavors of black stone fruit mix with good midmouth moderate tannins and good acidity, leading to a balanced, clean finish. The 2000 vintage received a bronze medal at the San Francisco International Wine Competition. Match with *arroz con pollo*, or grilled quail.

Chardonnay: 100% varietal, from San Antonio de las Minas. Low temperature slow fermentation is started in stainless steel; the final month is finished in temperaturecontrolled French oak barrels, followed by an additional two months of barrel aging and 100% malolactic fermentation. Very light straw color, with aromas of pippin apple, pear, and honey. Continued apple-like flavors in a soft mouth feel, yet prominent acid components give it a good body, with a clean, slightly hot finish. Drink this today with chicken salad, or Puerto Nuevo lobster.

Chenin Blanc: 100% varietal, from the Valle de las Palmas. Low temperature slow fermentation totally in stainless steel is followed by controlled temperature cold stabilization. Light straw/green color, with aromas of banana, mango, and citrus are followed by ripe citrus flavors and good acid balance. This dry version fills the mouth and shows a lingering finish that's smooth and clean. Enjoy with ceviche, or grilled chicken breasts with fruit salsa.

Fernando Martain in his wine cellar.

Chapter 6

the Valley Wineries

Valle de Guadalupe's cooling marine mists provide a moderating climate for the production of fine wines.

Casa Pedro Domecq

A fountain with gigantic clay amphorae greet visitors to the wine cellar and tasting room at Casa Pedro Domecq.

The Essentials

Address: Hwy 3 at Km 73

Telephone: 646-155-2249/54

Fax: 646-623-8387

Email: none

WebPage: www.domecq.com.mx

Established: 1972

Owners: Grupo Allied-Domecq

Winemaker: Jose Luis Durand Zuñiga

Tasting Room: Winery tour/tasting M-F 9am-3pm, Sat. 9am-1pm

Current Production: 3.4 million liters/yr

Vineyard Size: 1,200 acres (480 hectares) in 3 different Baja valleys

Grape Varieties

Red: Cabernet Sauvignon, Tempranillo, Barbera, Grenache, Merlot, Nebbiolo, Petite Sirah, Zinfandel

White: Chardonnay, Chenin Blanc, French Colombard, Sauvignon Blanc, Riesling

Winery History

In 1972, Pedro Domecq, the huge producer of El Presidente Brandy, founded the first modern commercial winery in the Valley. Vides del Guadalupe, as it was then named, was built at the northern end of the Valley beside Highway 3 at Km 73. Manager Luis Angel Cetto, who would soon build his own winery across the street, designed the facility and hired Italian trained Camillo Magoni as the winemaker. The winery façade is impressive, dominated by a gigantic fountain of stone barrels. Inside is a large tasting room whose windows offer impressive views of the valley.

Enologist José Luis Durand Zúñiga of Vinos Domecq.

By 1973 the winery was shipping wines labeled as originating in the Valle de Calafia, a name that the winery gave to their portion of the Valle de Guadalupe. It was a clever move, for it distinguished Domecq from other Valley producers, and at the same time introduced a distinctive regional appellation. The ancient name of the legendary Amazon queen Calafia (from the Greek *kali*, "beautiful" and *ornix*, "bird"... presumably because she was beautiful and traditionally accompanied into battle by 500 flying griffins), from which "California" was derived, reminded consumers of their prehistory "roots." Further land acquisitions to the north and in the Valle de San Vicente to the south permitted them to expand production dramatically. Domecq's business plan was to make inexpensive wines under a variety of labels, and to produce a lot of it. The plan worked very well. Domecq wines are distributed under many labels including Padre Kino, Los Reyes, Calafia, and the X-A line. Although very few of the surrounding vineyards are used in their wine production today, Domecq is one of the two largest producers of table wines in Mexico (across the road neighbor Cetto is the other). Together, they account for nearly eighty percent of the 1.6 million cases of wine Mexico produces annually. More recently Domecq has begun to improve and expand its line of premium wines: Reservada and X-A. Former winemaker Ron McClenden, and current Chilean winemaker Jose Luis Durand have been encouraged to set standards of quality that bode well for the future. The winery eventually was renamed Domecq Winery, and now goes by the friendlier Casa Pedro Domecq, or simply "Domecq."

Winemaker Notes

"Domecq wines fall into three categories: Premium Wines, Fine Wines, and Wines of Lower Alcohol Content. The Premium line is oriented to achieve the highest level of quality possible, starting with small lots selected from all over the country, and treated with vinification processes that will fulfill their individual potential. The Fine Wines line is oriented to wines of varietal character with personalities defined by the terroir. The objective of Wines of Lower Alcohol Content (Vinos de Baja Graduacion) is to achieve wines with full aromas and color, with a style resembling French Beaujolais. They must be very fresh and lively, with a light body and easy to drink, wines that can be included in any occasion. At the same time they are competitive because of their favorable quality to price ratio."

Vineyard and Fermentation Techniques

The Premium Line includes the Reservada and Chateau class of wines. The whites are collected at 22 to 23 degrees Brix sugar, macerated for twelve hours at 5 to 7 ºC, cold stabilized in stainless steel tanks at 15 to 20 ºC before placing in small wooden barrels for six months before bottling. The reds are harvested at 24 to 25 degrees Brix, before maceration and placed directly in small wooden barrels. The Fine Wines line includes the XA and Tinto Calafia wines. Their treatment is similar to that of the Premium line. The Vinos de Baja Graduacion line includes the Red and White Los Reyes and Padre Kino products. These are harvested at 22 to 23 degrees Brix, whites undergoing no malolactic fermentation, and both reds and whites are fermented in stainless steel and go directly into bottle.

The Wines

Cava Reservada: **A blend of their best** Cabernet Sauvignon **and** Merlot **grapes. After a traditional fermentation, it is aged for 18 months in French oak barrels followed by a minimum two years further maturation in bottle. Brick-red color; aromas of dried cherries, black pepper, vanilla, and oak follow through into mature earthy flavors of plum, toast, and dill. Mid tannins and moderate acidity balance in the mouth to provide tobacco-earth accents in the finish. Serve with beef Florentine or strongly flavored cheeses.**

Tinto Reserva Real: **A blend of** Cabernet, Barbera **and** Tempranillo. **Stainless steel fermented and aged in American oak, with further bottle aging prior to release. This unusual blend displays aromas of black cherries, green herbs, vanilla, and cedar, with flavors of cherry, chocolate, and herbs. The moderate tannins and significant acidity should match it well with** chiles en nogada, **or beef in mushroom sauce.**

Merlot Tinto X-A: **100% varietal. Ruby-red color, with aromas of red stone fruit, and hints of vanilla. Soft forward tannins and good acids provide a clean finish, while supporting flavors of black cherry and blackberry. Try it with lamb kebabs, or grilled salmon steak.**

Chardonnay X-A: **100% varietal. Totally fermented in French oak, and left** sur lies **for six months in barrel. Light straw color, with aromas of apple, peach, pineapple, butter, caramel, and vanilla. Flavors of tree fruit are well balanced by good acidity, and offer a clean finish. Good with grilled tuna salad, or fish tacos.**

Blanc de Blanc X-A: **100%** *Chenin Blanc,* **specially selected. Low temperature fermentation in stainless steel captures the fruity richness and aromatic character of the grape. The wine sees no oak, is bottled and released without aging. Very light straw color, the slight sweetness and acidity seem to intensify the fruit aromas and flavors while offering a clean lingering finish. Serve with apricot glazed ham, or as an appetizer.**

Blanco Reserva Real: **A blend of** *Chenin Blanc, Sauvignon Blanc* **and** *Riesling.* **Stainless steel fermented, with no oak treatment. Greenish straw color, with forward peach, grapefruit, and herbal aromas. The citrus flavors are full on the palate with a finish that is clean and long. Should be nice with fish in white wine sauce, or veal scaloppini.**

Critical tasters evaluate Domecq's many wines in the Tasting Room.

95

L. A. Cetto

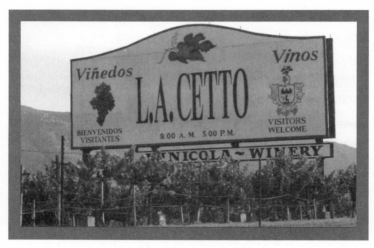

The entrance to L.A. Cetto, along Highway 3.

The Essentials

Address: **Hwy 3 at Km 73.5, Valle de Guadalupe (Tijuana: Cañon Johnson 2108, zona Central)**

Telephone: **646-155-2264 (Tijuana: 664-685-3031)**

Fax: **646-155-2269**

Email: none

Web Page: www.lacetto.com.mx

Established: **1974**

Owners: **Luis Alberto Cetto**

Winemaker: **Dr. Camillo Magoni**

Tasting Room: **7 days, 10:00 am to 5:00 pm; winery tours**

Current Production: **15,000 tons/year (840,000 cases)**

Capacity: **26 million liters**

Vineyard Size: **2,500 acres (1,000 hectares)**

Grape Varieties

Red: Cabernet Sauvignon, Petite Sirah, Nebbiolo, Zinfandel, Merlot, Malbec, Grenache, Sangiovese, Sirah, Petite Verdot, Tempranillo and Mourvedre.

White: Chardonnay, Sauvignon Blanc, Chenin Blanc, Viognier and Muscat Canelli.

Winery History

The story begins in 1928 with engineer Angelo Cetto, who two years earlier arrived in Tijuana from his native Italy, founded a wine-bottling business and named it Bodegas Cetto. After Prohibition he promptly purchased the property where the office and bottling facility were located, ensuring a centralized urban facility which remains their headquarters today. In 1945 Angelo's eldest son, Luis Ferruccio, began exporting fortified and table wines to Mexico City by first trucking them down to the port of Ensenada. The cases then were loaded on ships that traveled south to Cabo San Lucas at Baja's tip and across to Acapulco, where they were unloaded for land shipment to Mexico City. In those days, the main road to the interior of Mexico had not been built, so commercial travel was slow and painful (especially for wine).

By the fifties the Cettos were looking to the Valle de Guadalupe as a further source of grapes, and in 1957 changed their name to Productos de Uva ("Grape Products"), S.A. de C.V. In 1960 the Cetto family acquired their first 250 acres (100 Ha) in the Valley. This was followed in 1968 by the purchase near Tecate of the El Escondido Ranch, with 180 acres (73 Ha) of dry-farmed Zinfandel vines. This vineyard had been planted in 1930 with cuttings imported from the Escondido area of Southern California (The latter was an early source of Zinfandel for bulk wine production in California, and remains a limited "old vines" source for some of the wineries in California's Temecula area.). After 1970, the properties became the sole ownership of Don Luis Agostín Cetto, Don Angelo's son, who continued to acquire land and plant new vineyards.

With the founding of Domecq's first (and only) Mexican winery in 1972, Sr. Cetto was enlisted by the giant brandy company to design, build and manage their new facility at the northeast end of the Valley. Soon afterward he hired a young Italian winemaker named Camillo Magoni to be his head winemaker. Magoni had begun his training at Alba, in northern Italy's Piedmont region, followed by a study of clonal varieties of the *Nebbiolo* grape at Nino Negri in northern Lombardy. Having met Magoni during a trip back to Italy, Don Luis now persuaded him to come to Mexico and join the new winery.

1974 saw the founding of Cetto's own Vinicola L.A. Cetto, located almost directly opposite Domecq on Highway 3. With him came Magoni, among whose first tasks was the selection of about 2500 acres (1000 Ha) for planting to numerous classic varieties, such as *Cabernet Sauvignon*, *Merlot*, *Petite Sirah*, and among the whites: *Chardonnay*, *Sauvignon Blanc* and *Chenin Blanc*. Don Luis and Camillo wisely agreed that the Valley's Mediterranean climate was conducive to the cultivation of Italian varieties as well, and several of the vines introduce by Ferro thirty years earlier [See chapter on Valle de Guadalupe] were included in the selection. Diversified production began in 1979, and the first bottles bearing the name "L.A. Cetto" appeared in 1983. In 1990 further introduction of red varietals was made, including *Syrah*, *Sangiovese*, *Petite Verdot* and *Malbec*, as well as the new white varietal, *Viognier*. Systematic acquisition of vineyard property has brought their total management holdings to about 2,500 acres (1000 Ha), distributed among the regions of Guadalupe, Tecate, San Vicente and San Antonio de Las Minas [See chapter on Other Valleys].

Camillo Magoni, Director of Winemaking at L.A. Cetto.

Today, Cetto is Mexico's largest producer of table wines with sales of over 840,000 cases annually, plus a considerable quantity of sparkling wine, wine coolers and bulk wine. They export currently to 29 countries including the United States, Italy, France, United Kingdom, Spain, and Canada. In addition to L.A. Cetto, their brands include: Don Luis Seleccion, Chauvenet, Marques del Valle, Santa Cecilia (export), and Castillo del Rhin.

Winemaker Notes

Winemaster Camillo Magoni insists that a primary goal for him has always been to "make wines with personality." He adds, "Of course it is our goal to make very good wines, that is, the most sophisticated, but we recognize that we (Mexican wineries) cannot (yet) command top prices in the world market." Regarding suitability of vineyard selection, Magoni states, "I have always been convinced that the Mediterranean climate of our Valley is especially friendly to grapes such as *Nebbiolo* and *Petite Sirah,* but we are also experiencing considerable success now with such classic varietals as *Cabernet Sauvignon* and *Chardonnay.* However, I am an experimentalist and love to try many different varietals including *Viognier* and *Sangiovese,* as well as new blends such as *Cabernet Sauvignon* with *Syrah.*"

Vineyard & Fermentation Techniques

As described by Camillo Magoni, "The old vineyards are on their own rootstock, but new plantings are grafted (onto disease-resistant rootstock). The vineyard orientations are east-west or north-south. The trellis system originally used was T-trellis, but proved to be a poor one. Current practice is to use vertical cordon, open lyre, or head prune systems. Planting density is about 2780 plants per hectare, or 3700 per hectare when trellised with an open lyre system. Enological practices are typical of the temperate zone. They start at the vineyard with careful control on ripening; we control yield, bunch-light exposure (canopy management), polyphenols, sugar, acidity pH and flavor by tasting before harvesting. Dry farming or drip irrigation is practiced. All grapes are hand picked with average yields of 3-4 tons per acre for the reservas. The winery buildings are insulated and temperature controlled year-round; permanent controlled-temperature during fermentation is 14°C for whites and 25°C to 30°C for reds. Crushers are the latest generation, destemming is a gentle operation with variable-spaced rollers. The presses are of the pneumatic (bladder) type. We use selected yeast, low or no SO_2 (sulfur dioxide) before fermentation on the barrel-fermented whites and all reds, and none on the tank-fermented whites. For whites only the first 55% of the juice is retained. All wines are cold stabilized and filtered but not centrifuged. The reserve reds (*Cabernet Sauvignon* and *Nebbiolo*) receive long maceration times and are aged one year in French oak barrels and at least two years in bottle before release to the market."

The Wines

Today's LA Cetto wines, having been awarded over 75 medals since 1992, demonstrate across the board many of the characteristics judged to be desirable in the world wine market. Their *Petite Sirah, Nebbiolo* and *Cabernet Sauvignon* have received the most attention, but others on the list are moving up. Whether it was due to their image as the big guy on the block or their large stable of wine offerings and labels, the perception persisted among some that bigness was not synonymous with quality. Just as Gallo has shown that determination and effort, when properly directed, can produce premium-quality wines even by a huge winery, the largest winery in Mexico has demonstrated more recently that they are willing to invest what is necessary to move into the realm of super-quality wines. Their newest line of reserve wines demonstrates that dedication and commitment.

Don Luis Cetto Seleccion Reservada: First released in 2002, this series of wines named in honor of the winery's owner, are the first vineyard-designated wines offered by Cetto. Located in the eastern part of the Valley, the vineyards are named "Viña Alegre," "El Encinal," and "Las Bellotas." These wines signal Cetto's move into the premium wine market, with the three reds undergoing traditional vinification methods including extended maceration, and spending one year in small oak barrels prior to further aging in bottle.

Terra: A classic *Bordeaux* blend of 50 percent *Cabernet Sauvignon,* 30 percent *Merlot,* and 10 percent each of *Malbec* and *Petite Verdot.* Ruby color, complex aromas of red and black fruit with velvety balanced flavors supported with a firm structure of medium forward tannin, ends with a clean lasting finish. A serious wine capable of aging and improving further for several years. Serve with steak Florentine or barbecued leg of lamb.

Concordia: A unique blend of 60 percent *Cabernet Sauvignon* and 40 percent *Shiraz,* it displays an intense ruby color, with characteristic aromas of black fruit, tobacco, and spice. Medium full-body, good balance, soft mid-palate tannins and a clean extended finish. Delicious today with grilled meat or Cornish hens, but capable of holding for at least 2-4 more years.

Merlot: 100 percent varietal. An intensely ruby color, and good aromas of black cherries and smoke follow through with cherry/chocolate flavors and soft forward tannins in the mouth. Good balance and a nice velvety feel lead into a smooth lingering finish. Serve with *carne asada* or chicken *mole.*

Viognier: 100 percent varietal vinified and fermented in stainless steel tanks at 13°C (55°C). An initial impression of subdued varietal fruit opens up upon warming in the glass to reveal inviting white peach and pear aromas, followed by a clean citrus and crisp acid mouth-feel. As this young vineyard mtures, wines produced from it should exhibit more complex flavors and aromas. The refreshing, lingering finish makes you want a second glass. Try with light appetizers or lobster tacos.

Other Reserve Wines (100% varietal)

Cabernet Sauvignon Reserva Privada: 25-day fermentation and maceration followed by French oak aging for 12-16 months and bottle-aged for three years before release. A tawny-garnet color, aromas of rose, tobacco, tea and sweet cherries followed by astringent dried cherry and spice flavors, moderate forward tannins and a persistent yet clean finish. An elegant wine that pairs well with *beef bourguignon* or aged cheeses. International medal winner.

Nebbiolo Reserva Limitada: 15-20 day fermentation followed by 12-18 months in French oak and at least 2 years in bottle before release. The structured 1997 was held for six years before release and shows typical varietal color of brilliant garnet, with aromas of rich earth, ripe dried plums, vanilla and wood. Complex red stone fruit and hints of forest flavors balance with moderately structured mid tannins to produce a nicely rounded spectrum of mouth-filling flavors that linger on the finish. An excellent example of a New World *Nebbiolo,* and a delicious complement to grilled meats or *funghi porcini risotto.* International medal winner.

Chardonnay Reserva Privada: Fermented 7 months *sur lie* in French oak barrels, aged a further 7 months in French oak and six months in bottle before release. Brilliant straw-gold color. Aromas of ripe peaches, pineapple, vanilla and toast are followed by complex apple and citrus flavors that drink with a full and round mouth sensation that persists in the long delicious finish. A big but balanced wine that will go well with richly sauced seafood or *tamales con pollo*. International medal winner.

Linea Classica (100% varietal)

Chardonnay: Fermented 25 days in stainless steel and bottle aged 6 months before release, this is the junior sibling of the above wine. Brilliant light straw in color, the apply pear nose plus mineral and pippin apple flavors shine through this laser-clean unoaked version. The fresh, slightly astringent finish adds to its appeal as an accompaniment to seared ahi tuna or chicken *fajitas*.

Petite Sirah: 25 days of tank fermentation plus six months in large oak casks with six months in bottle. Bright garnet color, berry and spice nose, followed by tart red cherry and black pepper flavors integrate with smooth, forward tannins and mild acidity to produce a lighter styled yet tasty version of this varietal. Good with grilled red meats or *chile verde*. International medal winner.

Cabernet Sauvignon: 15 days of tank fermentation plus one year in 225-liter oak barrels with six months in bottle. Ruby-garnet color with aromas of tobacco, cedar and dried plum; flavors of black cherry and pepper project a slight astringency and tartness combined with forward modest tannins. Good body and balance make for a satisfying finish. Suitable with red meat or tomato-based dishes. International medal winner.

Zinfandel: 15 days of tank fermentation plus six months in large oak casks with six months in bottle. Brilliant ruby red color, and raspberry-like aromas show modest varietal character. Berry flavors combined with light astringency and forward tannins provide a decent structure and a clean finish. Although not a powerhouse Zin, it shows its versatility by matching well with spicy tomato-based dishes or grilled hamburgers. International medal winner.

Fume Blanc: Stainless steel fermentation for 25 days at 13°C, no further aging. Light straw color, hints of hay, herbs and melon with clean varietal character. These flavors carry through in a full-bodied dry style showing good acidity, with a clean moderate finish. Serve with shellfish, goat cheese, or *bouillabaisse*.

Chenin Blanc: Stainless steel fermentation for 30-40 days at 13°C, no further aging. Brilliant very light straw color, with aromas of citrus fruits, mango and herbs. Lightly acidic, off dry but well balanced with citrus, apple and slight minerally flavors that finish very clean. Enjoy with fruit salad, chicken, grilled veggies or simply on its own.

Plant Manager Juaquin Leyva.

Associate
Enologist/
Winemaker
Christian
Mackay
Tepper.

Members of the Society of Wine Educators taste Cetto's commercial and experimental wines while enjoying the view from the
winery's hillside picnic area.

Monte Xanic

Entrance to the Monte Xanic winery just beyond the village of Francisco Zarco.

The Essentials

Address: **Approximately 2 miles south, beyond Francisco Zarco. Turn right at the marked gate.**

Telephone: **646-174-6155**

Fax: **646-174-6848**

Email: **mxanic@montexanic.com.mx**

Web Page: **www.montexanic.com**

Established: **1988**

Owners: **Multi-partnership**

Winemaker: **Dr. Hans Backhoff (also Director and Co Owner)**

Tasting Room: **By appointment. M-F 9:00-4:00 pm, Saturday 8:00-12:00**

Current Production: **40,000 cases**

Vineyard Size: **185 acres**

Grape Varieties

Red: Cabernet Sauvignon, Merlot, Cabernet Franc, Petit Verdot, Malbec, and Syrah.

White: Chardonnay, Sauvignon Blanc, Chenin Blanc, and Semillon.

Winery History

Winemaker Hans Backhoff earned his doctor's degree in food science from the University of Nottingham, England. After returning to Ensenada, where he had lived as a youth, Backhoff worked for a while in the food industry as a chemist. During this time he developed a local reputation as an accomplished amateur wine maker.

In 1987 a group of investors, including Hans, decided to start a small winery that would produce a limited quantity of premium wines, with Backhoff as a partner and winemaker. While visiting the Valle de Guadalupe, they found what they believed was the ideal site. Thus, 175 acres of vineyard land were purchased, located on the north side of the valley, near to the eastern end, just beyond the village of Francisco Zarco.

Because of their belief that *Bordeaux* varieties express the character of this land with refinement and distinction, the partners chose to focus their attention on making premium *Bordeaux*-type red and white wines. In addition, because of the success of *Chenin Blanc* and *Chardonnay* in the valley, these varietals also were included. A Russian Molokan family previously owned part of the vineyard, and some of these vines were forty years old. This allowed them to immediately make some of their wines with a complexity that only comes from using older vines.

The unusual name and logo for the winery came from a visit made by the partners after a spring rain. They found the valley covered with beautiful desert flowers. This prompted them to name the winery Monte Xanic, a combination of Mexican and Indian words loosely meaning "the first flower that blooms on the mountain after the rain."

Winemaker and Co-Partner Hans Backhoff of Monte Xanic.

Founded in 1988, the winery became an almost immediate success, with its super premium wines selling out, and case purchases commonplace by sophisticated wine consumers in Mexico City. Elsewhere, its recognition as the first prestige "Mexican boutique winery" has boosted sales, and exports now are about six percent. The Henry Wine Group currently distributes its wines, and a cooperative agreement with Chalone Wines makes them available wherever Chalone wines are sold.

Winemaker Notes

Hans Backhoff states that winemaking "decisions are part of the French concept of terroir, which is the interaction between climate, soil and the grape variety planted there. The basic principle of the Monte Xanic wine-making philosophy is to bring out the results of this interaction, making wines with great character and personality which are produced naturally in the vineyard." He further notes, "Everything a wine can ever be is in the grape. Through the vine the grapes absorb the characteristics of soil and climate; the grape interprets them while contributing its varietal character. While the characteristics of the vineyard are natural and cannot be reproduced by technology, it can be used to allow the grapes to develop their full potential. We have just released our first *Syrah* (500 cases) which we feel has a lot of potential here, since our weather is very similar to that of the Rhone Valley."

Vineyard and Fermentation Techniques

Backhoff explains, "We cultivate our vineyard with both traditional and modern techniques in order to obtain the maximum expression of our vineyard. One of the most important aspects is controlling yields, sacrificing volume for quality. Each vine is pruned to yield a limited number of grapes, but each one of these has a high concentration of flavors and aromas, which will be revealed in the wine. We also prune leaves and branches to reduce herbaceous aromas. Drip irrigation controls the amount of water that goes into the vineyard, and we protect the vines from birds with nets.

"To make our wines, we use the most advanced technology to create the ideal conditions during pressing, fermentation, ageing and bottling to allow the greatest development of what the grape contains. To prevent damage during harvest our

grapes are handpicked, placed in small baskets and immediately taken to the press. White grapes are picked at night, to
preserve freshness and avoid oxidation as much as possible.
We use a membrane press, which slowly extracts the juice at
low pressure. For red wines, we carry out two types of
fermentation; one takes place in a rotofermentor, which produces high extract of color and flavor. The other is the
traditional maceration with the pumping-over technique to
obtain good concentration and refinement."

The Wines

With its release in 2000 of the following two wines, Monte
Xanic has raised its goal of super premium wine production
another notch.

Gran Ricardo de Monte Xanic: Named in memory of one of
the winery's founders, this is a classic *Bordeaux* blend of 50%
Cabernet Sauvignon, and 25% each of *Merlot* and *Cabernet Franc.*
Harvest vineyard yield was only 2.8 tons/acre. Fermentation
to dryness yielded an alcohol level of 13.5% and total acidity of
0.6%. Selected from the best barrel lots of each, the wine was
aged for 22 months in new French oak barrels before bottle
aging in magnums for an additional four years prior to release.
Production is limited to 1,500 magnums per vintage. A deeply
garnet red color, its aromas are complex, with hints of black
stone fruits, vanilla, and oak. Flavors of black cherry, plum,
pepper, cassis and a hint of cedar are balanced by a firm
structure of acid and moderate forward tannins that leads into
a lingering finish. If you are holding a special party that calls
for a magnum at dinner, you might consider this one to drink
today with lamb, beef or aged cheeses. But if you want to plan

ahead, this also will continue to develop for a few more years. International silver medal.

Calixa Cabernet Sauvignon: **From the Nahua Indian words for "from the house of Xanic," this 100%** *Cabernet Sauvignon* **comes with a dramatic black label stamped with a gold seal showing the Nahua hieroglyph "2 ácatl," symbol of the new fire of the Aztecs, and renewed hope for the future. With a vineyard yield of about three tons per acre, the grapes were fermented for ten days followed by 8 months in new French oak barrels. The wine is brilliant deep red-purple, with rich varietal aromas of raspberry, strawberry and cherry, integrated with hints of cassis and toast. Berry, dark chocolate, spice and oak flavors are evident, with soft mid-palate tannins balancing the acidity, to produce a pretty wine of medium body and clean, slightly chalky finish. Should match well with grilled red meats, duck, and ripe cheese. Drinking nicely now, but look for further complexity with a few more years of age.**

Cabernet Sauvignon: **100% varietal, barrel aged for 18 months in new French oak. Deep red, with complex aromas of berries and dark stone fruit, vanilla, chocolate and pepper. The flavors are balanced, full of red fruit and medium acid; moderate tannins provide a good mouth-feel and structure. The wine finishes cleanly with complex, long flavors. Matches well with red meats such as** *carne asada* **as well as chicken in mushroom sauce. Multiple medal winner.**

Merlot: **100% varietal, barrel-aged for 18 months in new French oak. Deeply extracted, dark blue-purple color, a complex varietal mix of cherries, plums and strawberries blend** with toast, chocolate and vanilla aromas. The fruit carries over into the mouth, blending with soft mid-palate tannins, and sprightly acid to produce a lovely soft texture and long finish. Very good with grilled beef, lamb, and salmon. Multiple medal winner.

Cabernet Sauvignon y Merlot: 60% *Cabernet Sauvignon,* 20% *Merlot,* 10% *Cabernet Franc,* and 5% each *Malbec* and *Petit Verdot.* Vineyard yield is less than 3 tons/acre; barrel-aged for 18 months in new French oak. Deeply extracted, dark blue-violet color, this ultimate five-varietal *Bordeaux* blend displays a complex set of aromas, including red and black stone fruit, pepper, chocolate and vanilla. Oddly, this super blend seems to reduce the characteristic *Cabernet* flavors while intensifying the sense of complex ripe fruit. These blend nicely with a good backbone of moderate mouth filling tannin, showing a long, slightly hot finish. Delicious with beef, lamb and game dishes in rich mushroom-based sauces, or with an aged cheese. Multiple medal winner.

Chardonnay: 100% varietal, vineyard yield of 2.3 tons/acre, barrel fermented at 24 brix, 100% malolactic fermentation, six months *sur lie* in new French oak barrels, alcohol 13-14%. This wine shows a light straw color, with intense, complex aromas of pineapple, ripe peaches, butter, and a hint of vanilla. Smooth flavors of rich baked apple, butterscotch, and peach, balanced with sufficient acid, provide a full-bodied wine, supported by a clean lingering finish. Drink with deep-fried calamari, or creamy sauced dishes. Multiple medal winner.

Calixa Chardonnay: This second new wine under the Calixa label sports a more tailored design apropos of its contents. 100% varietal, stainless steel fermented at 22 brix and 50-

55°F, followed by about one week in new oak barrels before bottling. This simpler approach than that undergone by the previous wine nevertheless has produced a delicious new look style. Very light straw color, showing apple and pear aromas, followed by fresh pear and peach flavors, it is balanced by crisp fruit acids and a clean finish. Not one to ponder, it should be nice with crab enchiladas or fish tacos.

Chenin Blanc Reserva, **Rancho Siete Leguas:** 100% varietal, vineyard yield of less than 2 tons/acre, stainless steel fermentation to dryness and storage until spring following the harvest, no malolactic fermentation or barrel aging, alcohol 13%. This is the winery's first vineyard-designated wine, reflecting their belief in this neglected varietal. It is an amazing wine, pale straw, showing clean, fresh floral and fruit aromas of apples, pears, lemongrass and honey, with balanced fruit flavors in a crisp acid mouth feel, and a varietally appropriate slight bitter finish. Serve with fish, shellfish, and sautéed chicken.

Chenin Colombard: **95%** *Chenin Blanc* and **5%** *Colombard;* all stainless steel treatment, no malolactic fermentation, 0.6% residual sugar. This lightweight junior brother of the previous wine is a pleasant if not serious quaffer. Pale straw color, its strength is its charming nose of apple, banana, honey and citrus. A high acidity allows a fairly crisp set of fruit flavors to show without an overly soft finish. Good as an appetizer, with fruit salad, and chicken or light fish dishes.

Viña Kristel: **80%** *Sauvignon Blanc* and **20%** S*emillon;* vineyard yield 4 tons/acre, stainless steel fermentation to dryness, 100% malolactic fermentation, 3 months in French oak barrels, alcohol 12-13%. Brilliant light straw color; this wine's emphasis is on aromas of melon, mango and pear, followed by hints of butterscotch and vanilla. Although the *Sauvignon* profile is subdued, this dry *Bordeaux* blend lends a nice structure to the crisp citrus notes in the mouth that lead into a clean, slightly herbal, astringent finish. Many possibilities here; try with cheese fondue, shellfish, spicy dishes, including chicken, or as an appetizer. Multiple medal winner.

Chenin Blanc Cosecha Tardia: 100% *Chenin Blanc;* all stainless steel fermentation, no malolactic fermentation, 1.9% residual sugar, alcohol 13%. This lovely, slightly late harvest wine shows again the versatility of *Chenin Blanc* when properly handled. Medium straw color, it displays attractive aromas of honey, apple, and floral overtones. The slightly sweet peach and apple flavors are accompanied by a modest *petillance*, and balanced by good acidity, and an acceptably bittersweet finish. Try this with a mature cheese, and sweet-sauced dishes such as chicken *mole*, and duck *a l'orange*.

Interior of Monte Xanic with barrels and stainless steel fermentation tanks.

Chateau Camou

Chateau Camou from the entrance road. Note the large boulders on the hillside. (Courtesy: F. Favela)

The Essentials

Address: **Approximately 2+ miles south, beyond Francisco Zarco. Turn right at the marked gate.**

Telephone: **646-171-9300**

Fax: **646-176-0676**

Web Page: **www.chateau-camou.com.mx**

Established: **1995**

Owners: **Ernesto Alverez-Morphy Camou and Fernando Favela (Executive Director)**

Winemaker: **Dr. Victor Manuel Torres Alegre**

Tasting Room: **weekdays & Saturdays, 8 a.m.-2 p.m., closed Sunday**

Current Production: **15,000 cases/yr**

Vineyard Size: **approximately 200 acres**

Grape Varieties

Red: **Cabernet Sauvignon, Merlot, Cabernet Franc, and Zinfandel**

White: **Chardonnay, Sauvignon Blanc, and Chenin Blanc**

Winery History

This history began, ironically, with a visit to eventual neighbor Monte Xanic, by Ernesto Alverez-Morphy Camou. He had arrived from Mexico City to oversee one of his real estate ventures, and came to Monte Xanic at the invitation of the owners. Impressed with the facility and wine quality, Alverez-Morphy quickly decided that his next project would be to build his own state of the art winery. And what better location than next to Monte Xanic?

Thus in 1986 he purchased about 1200 acres in a nearby section of the Valley called Cañada del Trigo (Canyon of Wheat). He named the future winery, Chateau Camou, after his mother's maiden name. After planting only 100 acres the first year, about 50 more have been added with an annual expansion of about 12 percent anticipated.

Enologist and Partner Victor Manuel Torres Alegre worked towards his doctorate in the Institute of Enology at the University of Bordeaux, France. Returning to Mexico, Victor Torres was hired by Chateau Camou to be its winemaker and production manager. With fifteen years of wine making experience and French influenced, Torres has placed his stamp on the wines and design of Chateau Camou.

Starting in 1991, construction of the winery has been slow, although the plan was clear from the start. In a mission-style building, the newly picked grapes enter through a huge door patterned after one seen in an old Baja mission. It also appears on the wine label. A state of the art winery, its multilevel gravity flow operation has the grapes being brought in to the top level, with final barrel storage at the lowest level. "Wine quality was the first priority," said executive director Fernando Favela, "then came the tasting room."

Winemaker Notes

Victor Torres has said, "We are striving day-in day-out to attain a single goal: creating great wines in Mexico...every decision we make is aimed at achieving excellence in this marvelous and complex art of converting grapes into wine."

Winemaker Victor Manuel Torres Alegre of Chateau Camou in the temperature and humidity controlled barrel room.

He states "Chateau Camou's vineyards originate from grafts of noble varieties from the Old Continent, to develop to their utmost under the Baja California sun."

Vineyard and Fermentation Techniques

"We have a passion for quality," Teeres adds, "and take great pains to insure using the fruit to its maximum. We have achieved an increase to 2,400 plants per acre, the arrangement of grapevines with lyre trellising, exhaustive vineyard mainte-nance, and meticulous single cluster hand harvesting, as well as our sophisticated system of pressing, handling the must by gravity, advanced fermentation methods and equipment." Care-ful humidity controls in the aging room and natural inducement of malolactic fermentation by careful temperature control are two further innovative techniques introduced at this winery.

The Wines

The winery's products are sold under three labels: "Château Camou," "Viñas de Camou," and "Flor de Guadalupe."

El Gran Vino Tinto: **64%** *Cabernet Sauvignon,* **21%** *Cabernet Franc,* and 15% *Merlot.* Stainless steel fermented after crushing without carbonic maceration, cold stabilized at 22-25 °C for 35-40 days longer, then aged in new French oak for 13 months, natural malolactic fermentation initiated by temperature control, and blended just prior to bottling. It is then kept an additional 15 months in bottle before release. A deep ruby red color, with sweet-tart blackberry, herbal, coffee, and spice aromas. Complex black fruit flavors blend with pepper and vanilla overtones in a mix of good acidity and supple yet structured tannins, to produce a long, tasty finish. Enjoy with *osso buco,* wild quail, or aged cheese. Multiple medal winner.

El Gran Vino Blanco: **98%** *Sauvignon Blanc* with a touch of *Chardonnay* and *Chenin Blanc.* 100% barrel fermented, showing complex varietal aromas as well as those of toast, hay, figs and honey. Aged in 80% new French oak barrels, with no malolactic fermentation, yet the wine displays crisp full-bodied flavors moving toward a touch of earthiness in the clean finish. A stylish new release from the 1999 vintage. Serve with grilled tuna or goat cheese with sourdough bread.

Chardonnay: 100% varietal, mixture of grapes from 60 year-old and from young vines. Fermented and aged in new French oak barrels for nine months, 100% malolactic fermentation. Golden straw color, with aromas of peach, mango, butter, honey, vanilla, and toast. Complex flavors of citrus and apple are balanced in a round, mouth filling and lengthy finish. Try with crab enchiladas, or fish in a cream sauce. Multiple medal winner.

Fumé Blanc: 100% varietal. Fermented and aged in new French oak barrels for twelve months. Yellow-green color, aromas of apple, peach, melon, guava, and toast blend nicely, while citrus, and peach flavors combine with a slight mineral sense and moderate acidity to provide good body and a lingering and clean finish. Match this with fish tacos, or stuffed rainbow trout. Multiple medal winner.

Zinfandel: A blend of 70% *Zinfandel* (grapes purchased from Bibayoff's 18 year old dry-farmed vineyard), 15% *Cabernet Sauvignon*, and 15% *Cabernet Franc*. Stainless steel fermented at 28-30 °C, with long maceration time for the *Cabernets* and short for the *Zinfandel*, then held for 35-40 days more at 22-25°C, before being moved to French oak barrels for ten months of aging. Malolactic fermenta-tion is initiated naturally by temperature control. A bright red-purple color, the fresh raspberry and cherry aromas mix with vanilla and spice to carry through into a blend of ripe berry, red cherry and spice flavors balanced nicely with soft forward tannins and crisp acidity. A great wine to serve with chicken *fajitas*, turkey *quesadilla* or grilled hamburger. Medal winner.

El Gran Vino Tinto de Zinfandel: 100% varietal from old vines. 28% Brix at harvest, the wine displays very ripe sweet plum and berry flavors with some heat from its 17% alcohol level. A surprisingly clean yet rich finish lingers, complement-ing the mouth-coating mid tannins. Drink after dinner as an alternative to port.

Blanc de Blanc: **Blend of about 60%** *Chenin Blanc,* **25%** *Sauvignon Blanc* **and 15%** *Chardonnay.* The *Chenin Blanc* is fermented in a stainless steel tank, while the other two wines are fermented in new French Oak Barrels and aged for 7 months. A light straw color, with deep aromas of fresh pineapple, peach, guava, citrus and apple. Flavors of fresh fruit dominate with good acid balance and a slight hint of sweet oak. The finish is clean and long. Try as an aperitif, with a fruit salad or *cóctel de mar.* Multiple medal winner.

El Gran Divino: **Blend of 60%** *Chardonnay* **and 40%** *Sauvignon Blanc.* A remarkable late harvest style, grapes having been picked at about 33 degrees Brix, and fermented in French oak to a residual sugar level of near 9 degrees Brix and 13 % alcohol. Straw-colored, with aromas of lemon zest, orange blossom and honey, it offers delicious lemon cake flavors in a rich and smooth mouth feel balanced by good acidity. A lingering finish with an acceptable hint of bitterness. Savor this with sweetened fruit desserts or by itself.

Partners Ernesto Alverez-Morphy Camou (left) and Fernando Favela Vara (right). The door in the background is an early Mission design featured on Chateau Camou's logo. (Courtesy: F. Favela)

Mogor-Badan

The Essentials
Address: **Km 86.5 Highway 3**
Telephone: **646-177-1484**
Fax: **646-177-1484**
Email: **abadan@cicese.mx**
WebPage: **none**
Established: **1986**
Owner: **Antoine Badan**
Winemaker: **Dr. Antoine Badan**
Tasting Room: **by appointment**
Current Production: **550 cases/yr**
Vineyard Size: **5.4 acres**

Grape Varieties
Red: **Cabernet Franc, Merlot, Cabernet Sauvignon, and Tempranillo**

White: **Chasselas**

Winery History
With its first wine grape harvest in 1986, Mogor-Badan became a winery. Located on the south central side of the Guadalupe Valley, at the foot of the Sierra Blanca, it lies between elevations of 350 and 800 meters. Henry and Clotilde Badan, émigrés from Switzerland, acquired the original ranch, El Mogor, on which the winery is located. They planted carob trees, harvested the existing olive trees, and embarked upon a pioneering life in their new home. Henry's son, Antoine, with a Ph.D. in oceanography from Oregon State University,

decided an additional career was in order and began making wine from the fifty-year-old vineyard. After replanting portions of the vineyard to more modern grape varieties, the ranch-winery is now a producer of wine, the first bottling occurring in 1986. In addition, the working ranch continues to produce grapes, carob, and organic produce (by Antoine's sister, Natalia), and raises cattle. The winery presently consists of a simple adobe barrel room adapted from an old barn. Some of the vinification still takes place at Cavas Valmar, but a fermentation room and a cellar are planned for completion by 2004.

Winemaker Notes

"A careful application of the very scarce water resources of this arid land allow us to grow the products of our ranch. The landscape is rugged, handsome, with granite boulders outcropping from large hills covered with chaparral and separated by valleys of California oak (*Quercus californianus*), all framed by perennially blue skies. Water is scarce but pure, as it flows lengthy paths through the peninsular granites.

"As in all great wine regions, grapevines and man combine with the soil and climate to express the exceptional character of the region through its fine wines. What is the secret of the Valley? It's the soil and the breeze... When there's El Niño, and 600 mm of rain (24 inches) it's perfect Bordeaux conditions. But very stressed drought conditions have produced great wines. Soils at the Mogor-Badan vineyard are of shallow and compact clay, overlying deep strata of decomposed granite, which result from the erosion of the peninsular batholith. Rolling hills ensure good drainage and a spartan but diverse soil profile, in which the vine roots must dig deep to extract the little moisture and precious mineral nutrients that give the wines their complexity."

Vineyard and Fermentation Techniques

"Mogor-Badan consists of 5.4 acres of grapes on a 50 year-old vineyard, formerly dry-farmed as gobelets. The vineyard is now trained in a 1 m high vertical canopy, composed of 5 to 7 spurs on a single Royat arm per plant, with new plants added to double the density. Varietal composition has been modified to 1.0 ha of *Cabernet Franc*, 0.9 ha of *Merlot*, and 0.3 ha of *Cabernet Sauvignon*, with an occasional *Syrah* or *Grenache* remaining from the old vineyard. Judicious applications of water ensure adequate crops of the highest quality; yields at El Mogor are limited through pruning and thinning to 5-6 tons, or about 25 hectoliters, per hectare.

"The main production consists of 350 cases of a deep, cherry to garnet red wine, with complex overtones and a very good aging potential. An early 1987 reserve recently tasted still showed many evolving complex tannins. Mogor-Badan also produces a very limited edition of *Chasselas del Mogor*, a dry fresh white wine with overtones of honey and straw, the only *Chasselas* wine on the continent."

The Wines

Chasselas del Mogor: **Although planted worldwide, and occasionally harvested as a table grape, *Chasselas* is by far the favorite white wine of Switzerland, where it is treasured for its freshness and mellow character as well as its low acidity. Some say that it may be the oldest cultivated varietal. This Mexican version is made from 100 % of the varietal, fermented entirely in stainless steel and bottled immediately afterward. Light** straw in color, a smoky aroma with hints of candied citrus, its soft acid feel shows some grapefruit flavor over a flinty, somewhat minerally finish. Only 200 cases made yearly. Try this with cheese fondue or some of the exceptional Baja California raw oysters.

Red Wine (Untitled): **A blend of** Cabernet Franc, Merlot **and** Cabernet Sauvignon. **G**arnet in color, aromas of red cherry, spice and hints of mushrooms and meat gradually develop with some time in the glass. Flavors of dried plums, sour cherries and spices combine with mouth-coating astringency and moderate-forward tannins. The wine finishes cleanly with some heat and a hint of oak. A few years of additional bottle age should develop a more harmonious blend of complex flavors and tannins. Serve with grilled leg of lamb or braised beef with mushroom sauce.

Winemaker and Owner Antoine Badan of Mogor Badan.

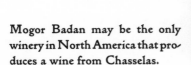

Mogor Badan may be the only winery in North America that produces a wine from Chasselas.

Vinos Bibayoff (Bodegas Valle de Guadalupe)

The Essentials

Address: Rancho Toros Pintos, Valle de Guadalupe
Telephone: 646-176-1008
Fax: 646-177-2722
Email: Bibayoff@telnor.net
Web Page: none
Established: around 1970
Owners: David Bibayoff Dalgoff
Winemaker: David Bibayoff Dalgoff
Tasting Room: Yes
Current Production: 1,500 cases/yr
Vineyard Size: 10-20 acres

Winery History

Interest in grape growing and wine making can be traced back to the first Russian Molokan communities whose members arrived in the Valley around 1906. Although these were largely wheat growers, subsequent immigrants, skilled in viticulture, planted vineyards for production of table grapes and wine. In the 1930's Alexie M. Dalgoff obtained a permit to make wine. By the early 1970's his grandson, David Bibayoff Dalgoff, had founded his own company, Bodegas Valle de Guadalupe, popularly known as Vinos Bibayoff. Although most of the grapes are sold off to other wineries, the company currently produces five estate wines as well as delicious Red Globe table grapes.

Located in the far southwestern end of the Valle de Guadalupe, visitors are advised to use caution while driving along the largely unmarked gravel road, whether approaching from Francisco Zarco or from Highway 3 at Km 92. A call to the winery to obtain specific directions is recommended. Although the trip should be taken slowly and not during periods of rain, once you have arrived, David Bibayoff will make your visit a charming and enjoyable one. The large sprawling front lawn is home to several huge trees, one with a swing that is difficult to resist sitting in and pleading someone to push to increasing heights. In the afternoon, cooling breezes that appear earlier in this part of the valley add to the ambience, and can persuade one that a hike up to the unassuming wine barn with a corrugated iron roof may not be necessary. A small family museum of Russian memorabilia may be visited on request.

Winemaker Notes

Although most of the grapes we harvest are sold to the local wineries, we save some of our best grapes to make our own estate wines. Today we use modern techniques to produce wines of the best quality.

Vineyard and Fermentation Techniques

The grapes are harvested at the end of August and during September. These are taken from vineyards adjacent to our winery in Rancho Toros Pintos, the name given to this portion of Valle de Guadalupe. This is a privileged zone with noble earth, cold nights and warm days, all necessary to give a good quality to the wines. All Bibayoff wines spend some time after fermentation in French oak barrels.

The Wines

Colombard: 100% varietal. Light straw color, closed fruit and aromatic aromas, off dry flavors of fruit and honey, low acid with clean finish. Serve with mixed fruit salad or *ceviche*.

Chenin Blanc: 100% varietal. Very light straw color, hints of white peach aromas, modest minerally fruit flavors with low acid structure and warm but clean finish. Drink with fresh stone fruits or melon.

Cabernet Sauvignon: 100% varietal. Light garnet color, ripe berry fruit aromas wrapped in weedy aromatic overtones. Straightforward cherry flavors show mid palate persistent tannins and a short but clean finish. Try with grilled chicken or beef burritos.

Nebbiolo: 100% varietal. Deep red in color, the aroma hints of varietal character with smoky plum and spice-pepper accents. Mouth-filling tannins dominate the straightforward stone-fruit flavors and harsh finish. May benefit from 2-3 years further aging. Drink with beef stew or *carne asada*.

Zinfandel: 100% varietal. Deep red purple color, aromas of dark berries and spices. Forward firm tannins dominate this intense set of berry/cherry and spice-infused flavors, ending with a clean but short finish. Set it aside a couple more years to bring this powerful wine into focus. Try with barbecued tri-tip steak or short ribs.

Winemaker and Owner David Bibayoff Dalgoff of Vinos Bibaya-off, using a "thief" to re-move a wine sample from one of his bar-rels.

Viña de Liceaga

Viña de Liceaga. Its bright yellow color and close proximity to Highway 3 makes it clearly visible to all visitors.

The Essentials

Address: **Km 93 Highway 3**

Telephone: **Winery/Home 646- 155-3091**

Fax: **178-2922 (Ensenada)**

Email: **elibac@telnor.net**

Web Page: **www.vinosliceaga.com**

Established: **1993**

Owners: **Eduardo and Myrna Liceaga-Campos**

Winemaker: **Dr. Enrique Ferro**

Tasting Room: **Open weekends. Weekdays by appointment**

Current Production: **3,000 cases/yr**

Vineyard Size: **20 acres**

Grape Varieties

Red: Merlot, Cabernet Franc

Winery History

In 1982, Engineer Eduardo Liceaga acquired 50 acres of land on a ranch named El Paricutin near kilometer 93 on Highway 3 in the Valle de Guadalupe. In 1983 he planted 10,000 vines at this site, near San Antonio de las Minas. These vines however were table grape varieties, and in 1991 Liceaga decided to graft over to wine grapes and begin to make exclusively red premium wines. Although wine production began in 1993, grafting was not completed until 1998, with a final field composition of 60% *Merlot* and 40% *Cabernet Franc*. Liceaga purchased new equipment in 1998 in order to make his red wines on site. More recently, they completed a strikingly yellow building to house the winery. Nearby is Eduardo and Myrna Liceaga's new hacienda, decorated in complementary shades of blue and yellow. Although current annual production is about 2,500 cases, they plan to reach an ultimate vineyard capacity of 10,000 cases.

Winemaker Notes

Winemaker Enrique Ferro comments, "Our harvest is always in October/November...later than elsewhere in the Valley, allowing us longer hang time and greater flavor development."

Vineyard and Fermentation Techniques

The vineyard is at an elevation of 700 feet, with largely clay/sandy soil. Plant density is 12x7. All the wines undergo fermentation in either two 5,000 liter or two 17,500 liter stainless steel tanks. Temperature is held at no more than 30 degrees C for 23-25 days, with twice-daily pump over. New French and American oak is used each year. Barrel aging of each wine is maintained separately, with final blending completed after at least one year in oak.

The Wines

Merlot Gran Reserva: 80% *Merlot*/20% *Cabernet Franc,* harvested from the first grafting made in 1991. Aged in new oak barrels for 14-16 months, followed by about 8 months in bottle prior to release. Very dark red color; rich varietal aromas of cherries, prunes, and violets, blended with spicy scents of oak, coconut and vanilla. Soft mid-forward tannins and adequate acidity provide good structure, and complex, ripe black-fruit flavors offer a pleasing mouth feel and balance, leading to a clean long finish. Tempting to drink now, but may develop further complexity over several more years. Try with grilled salmon or lamb shanks *adobo*. Silver medal winner.

Merlot: 90% *Merlot*/10% *Cabernet Franc.* Traditional temperature controlled stainless fermentation, aged in oak barrels one year, followed by bottling and release. Dark ruby color, with varietal aromas of black cherries, berries and herbs. Its flavors display bright, ripe stone fruits and blackberries, with hints of wood; medium acidity and mid-soft tannins add good structure and a pleasant cherry finish. The 1999 vintage received a silver medal at the San Francisco International Wine Competition. Should go well with grilled chicken or *carne asada*.

Cabernet Franc: 100% varietal. Stainless steel fermented and barrel aged for one year before bottling and release. Ruby color with red-orange edges, the cherry and spice aromas comple-ment the ripe black cherry and plum flavors and structured acidity, while leading to an astringent but clean finish. Try with roast duck or chicken *mole*.

Consulting Enologist Enrique Ferro (left) and Owner-Director Eduardo Liceaga Campos (right) in the estate vineyard.

Casa de Piedra

Casa de Piedra and surrounding estate vineyard.

The Essentials

Address: **93.5 Highway 3, San Antonio de las Minas, Baja California**

Telephone: **646-178-2173**

Fax: **646-174-0881**

Email: **cpiedra@telnor.net**

Web Page: **www.vinoscasadepiedra.com**

Established: **1997**

Owners: **Hugo and Alejandro D'Acosta**

Winemaker: **Dr. Hugo D'Acosta**

Tasting Room: **yes, on appointment**

Current Production: **approximately 1,000 cases/yr**

Vineyard Size: **approximately 2 acres (~ 1 hectare)**

Grape Varieties

Red: **Cabernet Sauvignon, Tempranillo.**

White: **Chardonnay**

Winery History

After studying agricultural engineering at the University of Mexico, Hugo D'Acosta received his Ph.D. in enology and winemaking at Montpelier, France. Further study at Turin, Italy led to a time in Napa at Chappellet Vineyards. Former winemaker at Bodegas Santo Tomas, Hugo and his brother Alejandro began Casa de Piedra in 1997. The original intent, says Hugo, was "to produce an excellent wine for the enjoyment of the group of people whose interest and enthusiasm lay in the initiation of the winery." Designed and built by Alejandro, the stone farmhouse-like structure is deceptively charming in appearance when approached from the road. Inside however, it is an intimate state-of-the-art winery equipped with small capacity, computerized stainless steel tanks with programmable pump-over, a semi-gravitational system, and underground caves, storing barrels and bottled wine for aging. Surrounding the winery is a small vineyard planted to *Chardonnay*.

Winemaker Notes

"At Casa de Piedra, we have endeavored to make our 'Signature Wine' using the grapes from the area and its diverse microclimates. Utilizing the latest technology combined with the expertise and sensibility of our winemakers, we have attained a level upon which each bottle exclusively reflects the personality of the land." Winemaker D'Acosta notes "three harvests after the initiation of this project, we could detect the different characteristics of each year's vintage, expressing the philosophy of the Casa de Piedra, that each year the wine will be agreeably unique." His *Chardonnay is* "made with the inten-tion of expressing the pure character of the grape." This is achieved by avoiding "the addition of wood or any other technique that might distract the personality of the fruit."

Vineyard and Fermentation Techniques

Chardonnay grapes are harvested from a small estate vineyard adjacent to the winery planted at a density of 10,000 per hectare; most red grapes are from a twenty-year old vineyard in the San Vicente Valley planted at 4,000 vines per hectare. Both sources are largely dry-farmed.

During dry years, such as 2002, the wines are put through a short maceration period of less than 24 days, but in wet years the maceration period is extended. In 2001 the reds were allowed 15-30 day maceration with five automated half-hour "push downs" of the cap and pump-overs per day at a controlled temperature of 23-24 degrees C. Our *Chardonnay* undergoes no grape skin contact. We harvested the 2001 vintage at about 20 Brix sugar and fermented the juice to 3.3 pH and 7.5 total acidity at low temperature in order to keep the character of the grape.

We use half French and half U.S. oak barrels (new and 1-year old) from three different coopers. We find that our reds show best with at least some time in American oak and the *Chardonnays* usually better when exclusively aged in French oak.

The Wines

Because of the relative newness of the winery, creative and thoughtful experimentation still drives the evolution of the wines. Thus the following comments are not necessarily those of the most recent vintage, but may serve as a general guide to the characteristics to be found in these wines. At present only two wines are being made.

Vino de Piedra Tinto: **Approximately equal proportions of** *Tempranillo* **and** *Cabernet Sauvignon.* **Stainless steel fermented, finished in half French/half American oak barrels. Showing dark ruby color, the aromas of black cherry and blackberry mingle with a background of coffee and cedar. Balanced flavors of ripe berries and bittersweet chocolate blend with the soft mid and forward tannins to produce a smooth and deliciously long finish. Try this wine with carne asada, grilled salmon or aged cheese. Medal winner.**

Piedra de Sol Blanca: **100%** *Chardonnay,* **totally stainless steel fermented to dryness, 100% malolactic fermentation, and no oak used. Grapes are from an estate vineyard adjacent to the winery, planted at a density of 4,000 plants per acre. Very light straw color, aromas of pippin apples and pear, with refreshing flavors of apple, hints of orange blossom honey without bitterness; finishes lean but cleanly. Enjoy with mussels, or fish in a light cream sauce.**

Enologist and Co-Owner Hugo d'Acosta of Casa de Piedra, in his cellar.

Adobe Guadalupe Vineyard

Adobe Guadalupe Vineyards and Inn. The winery, vineyards, bed and breakfast, and stables are located at the end of an unpaved road behind the Molokan village of El Porvenir.

The Essentials

Address: Approximately 4 miles southwest of Francisco Zarco, past Chateau Camou. At the stop sign (adjacent to the Unidad Médica Familiar building) turn right and continue + mile more.

Telephone: 949-863-9776 (USA), 646-155-2094 (Mexico)

Fax: 949-955-1153 (USA), 646-155-2093 (Mexico)

Email: adobegpe@telnor.net

WebPage: http://www.adobeguadalupe.com

Established: 2000 (1st harvest)

Owners: Don and Tru Miller

Winemaker: Dr. Hugo d'Acosta

Tasting Room: Daily, with appointment

Current Production: **Limited**
Vineyard Size: **60 acres**

Grape Varieties

Red: **Cabernet Sauvignon, Merlot, Syrah, Nebbiolo, Grenache**
White: **Viognier**

Winery History

Adobe Guadalupe began as a Mediterranean-style hacienda, an impressive bed and breakfast inn with six carefully appointed guest rooms. In 1998 sixty acres of adjacent land were planted to eight varieties of wine grapes. A former tractor shed has become the unromantic but high tech winery. The first harvest was celebrated in 2000; the first wines were released in late 2002. Current emphasis is on red blends.

Winemaker Notes

Consulting winemaker Hugo D'Acosta comments that "Adobe Guadalupe wine is based on a production of red grapes picked mainly from our estate. Consequently we end up with compatible mixtures from different varietals. At present we have planted in our vineyards a broad selection of the following vines: *Syrah, Mourvedre, Cinsault, Grenache, Viognier, Tempranillo, Nebbiolo, Cabernet Sauvignon, Merlot, Cabernet Franc,* and *Malbec.* These grapes will give us a great spectrum of wines yielding us the ingredients to produce new and rich mixtures for our final product."

The first harvest year was 2000. The following four varietals were harvested at that time: *Cabernet Sauvignon, Merlot, Grenache,* and *Syrah.* These varietals were carefully blended, resulting in three final wines (See below).

Vineyard and Fermentation Techniques

The vineyard project is based on two main objectives: (1) To produce low yields and (2) to harvest grapes at their full maturity (every vineyard lot has its own maturity level). At present D'Acosta and Miller have planted a broad spectrum of grape types ranging from classic Bordeaux varieties such as *Cabernet Sauvignon, Merlot, Cabernet Franc* and *Malbec* to Italian (*Nebbiolo*) and Spanish (*Tempranillo*) varietals. Attention will focus also on Rhone grapes including *Syrah, Cinsault, Mourvedre, Grenache* and *Viognier*. Currently five acres of *Syrah/Shiraz* are planted to ten thousand plants, six acres are planted to twelve thousand *Cabernet Sauvignon* plants and five acres are committed to ten thousand *Merlot* plants. "The philosophy of our wines is very simple: We try to pick the fruit as ripe as possible when all the flavors of the grape are 'ready.' We work with medium to long maceration (enough extraction without risking the balances). Every grape and every year has its own maceration timing.

"For the aging process, we work with 1/3 new oak, 1/3 once used oak, and 1/3 twice used oak barrels. We use 40% American and 60% French oak barrels selected from different coopers. Again, our project is to produce blended wines from the broad spectrum of grapes that we have. We believe that the wine is made in the vineyard."

The Wines

Obviously seeking the "right" blend (that's one reason they call winemakers at successful Champagne houses, "master blenders", and why different wine blends show a variety of taste styles), the initial, 2000 vintage displays an interesting selection of grape pairings and style differences brought together by an overriding picture of very ripe fruit. Aged in barrels for 12 months.

Kerubiel: 70% *Syrah,* 30% *Grenache* (from Valle de San Vicente). Aged in barrels for twelve months. Dark purple red color, prominent stone fruit aromas, and very plumy ripe fruit flavors, with some back palate tannins apparent in the finish. Drink now or in next few years with meat loaf or spiced duck breast.

Gabriel: 60% *Merlot,* 40% *Cabernet Sauvignon.* Dark ruby color, aromas of ripe black cherry and blackberry co-mingle with hints of tobacco. Flavors of ripe berries and cherries blend with soft forward tannins to produce a clean short finish. Drink now with beef stew or grilled sausage

Serafiel: 60% *Cabernet Sauvignon,* 40% *Syrah.* Dark red color, rich fruit and peppery aromas. Intense flavors of ripe plum and berry play over forward soft tannins and acid, followed by a clean finish. Capable of aging several years. Should go well with beef ribs or beef adobo.

Owner Donald Miller (left) pours one of their estate wines for his field manager. Vineyards are visible through the winery window.

Vinisterra S.A. de C.V

The Essentials

Address: Currently in a converted house in San Antonio de las Minas, near Km 93 Hwy 3. Call for directions.

Telephone: 646-178-3350

Fax: none

Email: almerico53@yahoo.com.mx

Web Page: none

Established: 2002

Owner: Guillermo Rodríguez Macouzet

Winemaker: Cristoph Gaertner

Tasting Room: by appointment

Current Production: extremely limited

Vineyard Size: currently purchased grapes and leased vineyards

Grape Varieties

Red: Cabernet Sauvignon, Merlot, Syrah, Nebbiolo, Grenache

White: Chardonnay, Viognier, Rousanne

Winery History

This winery at present is so new that it has virtually no history. Ensenada businessman Guillermo Rodríguez Macouzet, who also owns Las Conchas, a seafood restaurant and bar in Ensenada, founded it in May 2002. Located in a converted house, they plan to build a $2 million winery nearby, producing 5000 cases, based on grapes from their own vineyards. Talented Swiss enologist Christoph Gaertner, formerly of Bodegas de Santo Tomás, will prove key to the operation.

Winemaker Notes

The wine of this area is "like Baja California, with full, ripe grapes, full body. It's an excellent region. It's like a treasure island. I have to let people know what we have. Nobody believes Mexico can produce such wine, but we know and believe in it. The idea of "Macouzet" is to present a Baja California originated, varietal wine with ripeness, elegance and depth. When time and our grapes are ripe we will be there with *Tempranillo/Grenache* and *Syrah/Mourvedre*. We are also planting experimentally *Cinsault*, and naturally, *Cabernet* and *Merlot*. White varieties are *Chardonnay*, *Viognier* and *Roussanne*."

Vineyard and Fermentation Techniques

Gaertner states "38 acres (15 hectares) of land have been purchased in San Antonio de las Minas, Santo Tomas Valley and in San Vicente. Last year (2002) we planted 1 hectare to grapes, this year 7 hectares, and next year another 7 will be planted. Meanwhile we made the 2002 harvest with grapes from contracted vineyards, managed by our criteria.

"The red wine is fermented by medium fermentation temperatures, undergoes malolactic fermentation in stainless steel, and aged in French oak after post fermentative maceration. The *Chardonnay* has a 3% of *Viognier* in it, is well bodied, balanced with mineralic nuances. There is only a part malolactic fermented, and it has never seen any wood."

The Wines

At this writing I have not tasted these wines, and can only list their composition. Last Fall a 1999 *Cabernet-Merlot* and a 2000 *Chardonnay* were released. A 2000 *Cabernet-Merlot* and a 2001 *Chardonnay* have been bottled and wait for release probably at end of 2003. The wines bear the label name "Macouzet." Since they are made largely from purchased grapes they may not reflect the grape character found in the eventual estate wines. There will also be a second label, "Chateau Domino", of less complex wines that are blends based on *Chenin Blanc* (whites) and *Tempranillo* (reds).

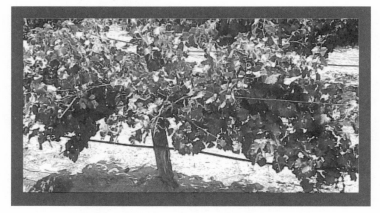

A vineyard of ripening grapes. Close examination reveals clusters of Chardonnay grapes among the characteristically shaped leaves of this classic varietal.

Part 3

Vintages & Grapes

Recent Baja Vintages

In addition to the effects of long-term climate, geographical location, soil condition, and a vineyard's slope, elevation and orientation to the sun, perhaps the most obvious factor affecting grape quality is the annual weather behavior. When a winemaker refers to a "vintage or cosecha" as good or bad, he/she invariably mentions rainfall, temperature and their seasonal variations as important determiners of the harvest's success. Some wine producing areas, such as California's Napa Valley, experience relatively little weather variation from year to year. Other regions, such as Germany's Mosel Valley and Italy's Tuscany region experience quite variable annual weather, and so-called "vintage charts" are published that indicate whether a year has been of good, poor or indifferent vintage quality. These, and many other important wine regions have reported such vintage charts for a long time. Although these reports are useful in judging whether an older wine that you plan to buy is going to taste as good as you hope, they are just that: a look backward, not a prediction of future harvest quality. The influence of weather on grape quality however is undeniable. In fact one expert on Bordeaux wines, Professor Orley Ashenfelter, has shown a consistent relationship between Bordeaux vintage quality and the average temperature/rainfall records reported at the Bordeaux airport. Even then the effect of weather will be different in its impact on white and red wine grapes, and needs to be evaluated separately.

Baja Norte however is a young area of serious commercial wine production, and such records are scarce at best. Only recently have vineyard temperatures been consistently re-corded and microclimates identified. However, even qualita-tive observations can be useful. The Association of Vitiviniculture of Baja California reported such a listing of recent vintages at their Fiestas de la Vendimia 2002. A portion of that information for the Valle de Guadalupe appears below.

1998: This was the year of El Niño, and it was rain, rain, rain. Almost 25 inches fell, lasting into late spring. Flowering and cluster formation was complicated and maturation developed under humid conditions. The summer was cooler and later than usual, however, producing very good acid balance. Some vineyards showed diseased fruit. The concentration of grapes was average, the range of aromatics good and the wines softer and of average ageability.

1999: This was the year of La Niña, characterized by a cold winter that decreased the incidence of plant disease and encouraged a more regular bud break. The rains were limited in quantity although of good distribution for the grape, with the latter achieving a high concentration of flavors in the fruit. The spring, unusually cold, slowed down the vegetative cycle of the plant, and produced lower yields, with a corresponding reduction in wine production. The beginning of summer was slow, and the coolness favored development of elegant grapes rich in aromas.

2000: The Millennium year presented this valley with a new climatological proposal for its grapes. The strange winter was not as cold as expected and was much drier than predicted (less than half of the average rainfall). Spring was cold and stimulated flowering but average-to-lower bunches of fruit. Summer began by struggling against a colder than normal sea, which beneficially extended the growing and maturation season and beautiful cool evenings. The summer was cool, although of variable humidity. The resulting wines were concentrated, with a good body balanced by a good aromatic charge.

2001: This year began with a very cold winter but with good rains, that delayed sprouting, but resulted in homogeneous and abundant results. Spring, with good humidity and few high temperatures favored flowering and cluster formation. Summer was hot but with cool evenings which assured a very good year. The wines are displaying great concentration and considerable aromatic character.

2002: This became the Year of the Drought, with miniscule rainfall and a cold winter. Vine growth was retarded below normal. At the end of April, daytime temperatures increased whereas nights became colder. The vineyards showed homogeneous flowering, although as summer arrived, the lack of rain found some winemakers, especially those with dry-farmed vineyards predicting lower yields. Several wineries however, produced excellent intensely concentrated wines.

The Grapes of Baja

Most grapes will grow anywhere, but the quality and style of the resulting wine is dependent upon many factors including grape type, soil, climate, vineyard management and winemaking technique. When left to their own devices, many tons of grapes can be produced from an acre of vines, and used to make a pleasant yet often nondescript wine. But to produce great wine from those grapes, one needs to start with high quality vines, plant them in a region of soil and climate that favors the grape type, limit production to a very few tons per acre through diligent vineyard pruning and water management, and finally, crush, ferment and age the juice with a sensitivity toward the wine that is being made. Only then will the resulting wine exhibit the complex aromas and transformed fruit flavors that are found and enjoyed in a premium wine.

Sometimes winemakers try to produce the best wine they can from the grapes they have inherited; others plant many types, and through what seems like trial and error discover which varieties best match the local environmental conditions. Still others seek out a site they know will favor the type of vines they wish to plant, and the style of wine they wish to make. What makes this an intriguing business is that the microclimates present in all the Baja valleys promise the possibility of premium wines to be produced from any of the following grapes. The ultimate success lies with the winemaker.

White Varieties

Chardonnay: The great white grape of *Burgundy* and *Champagne,* it performs best when grown in cool regions. It shows its versatility however, by making acceptable wines even when grown in more temperate zones. The wines can range from light greenish-straw to golden yellow in color, simple apple to complex tropical-fruit, butter, vanilla aromas, tart apple-like to complex buttery peach flavors, and mild to firmly astringent finishes, depending upon the winemaking style and vineyard location. It is grown in most areas of Baja.

Chasselas: A grape grown mostly in Switzerland, with very limited U.S. production. Mostly vinified to be a full, dry and fruity white wine. In France's Loire region it is blended with *Sauvignon Blanc.* Currently the only producer in Baja is Mogor-Badan, who produces a version with light acid and mineral-like overtones.

Chenin Blanc: Although an unappreciated grape in California (acreage fell from 31,000 to 18,000 between 1991 to 2001), while remaining the third most planted white wine grape, *Chenin Blanc* has long been a popular and widely planted variety in Baja. Here it is made in dry, slightly sweet, and dessert styles, with satisfying results. It is sometimes blended with *Colombard* to augment its aromatic character, which by itself suggests aromas of apples and honey. Flavors of grape-fruit and a lingering touch of minerality are often characteristic of this region's *Chenin Blanc.*

Colombard: Better known as *French Colombard* in North America. Despite a reduction in acreage from 56,000 to 40,000 in the past decade, it remains the second largest planted grape in California due to its ability to contribute significant acidity to jug wines. In Baja it is made in both dry and off-dry versions.

Sauvignon Blanc: Sometimes marketed under the name *Fume Blanc,* the vines frequently display vigorous growth and benefit from strict pruning during growing season (canopy management). It is a late maturing grape, which allows it to be harvested after most other varieties, which is a blessing for the winemaker with a limited number of fermentation tanks. In cool climates it shows a tendency towards making grassy, herbaceous flavored wines. In Baja's warmer regions, the flavors and aromas are more citrus-like, moving toward peach and pear, plus a characteristically mineral finish. Some winemakers polish the wine further by replacing the stainless steel with barrel fermentation and limited oak barrel aging. Also blended occasionally with *Semillon.*

Viognier: Remarkably, less than twenty years ago world plantings for this grape numbered less than eighty acres, almost entirely in France's northern Rhone, where it was blended into several red wines. California winemakers have become interested, and currently over two thousand acres are planted there alone. Increased interest regarding this grape in Baja suggests a future for it here as well. This often straw-tinted wine can display a range of full, spicy, aromatic aromas plus hints of blossoms such as violets. As with *Chardonnay,* this wine can vary in its persona, depending upon the winemaker's whim and vine maturity, sometimes showing considerable apple, apricot, or ripe peach flavors. It is best drunk while young.

Red Varieties

Barbera: Associated with northern Italy's Piedmont region, this was a favorite grape of the early Italo-California winemakers, such as Martini and Sebastiani, who used lots of it in their popular jug wines, but also made good examples of the single varietal. Its introduction to Baja in the early 1930s was by native Piedmontese Esteban Ferro of Bodegas de Santo Tomás. Intense red color, high acidity and modest tannins characterize the wine. In Baja the wines are often robust, with intense fruit flavors.

Cabernet Franc: This grape thrives in cooler regions than does its frequent blending partner, *Cabernet Sauvignon,* and thus seems to find a good home in the higher, cooler portions of Valle de las Minas, and in the higher microclimate segments of the larger valleys. The wine display a deep purple color and herbaceous, black cherry aromas when young.

Cabernet Sauvignon: A "noble" grape famous as one of the main varieties found in the red wines of Bordeaux. Known as a "hard" grape, it makes wines with firm tannins that often require at least five years to soften and develop flavor complexity. Since extended skin extraction is common in premium bottles of this varietal, 10-15 years is not uncommon a period to wait for the softening of the tannins. The key here is to balance the fruit content to insure that at tannin maturity there still remains enough fruit components to make the wine enjoyably flavorful and complex. Typical aromas and flavors include blackcurrant, blackberry, cherry, and mint.

Grenache: *Grenache* is widely grown in Spain, (where it is known under the name *Garnacha,* and is often blended with *Tempranillo*). It also appears as the main grape in the multi-varietal French red blend *Chateauneuf-du-Pape.* Although a high yield grape with good acidity, because of its characteristic pale red tint when allowed to overproduce, it is often blended with wines of more intense color and structure. If grown under more stressed, less fertile conditions, with strict pruning habits it is capable of producing interesting dark red wines of flavorful character often reminiscent of strawberries, cherries and raspberries. It also is capable of making a pleasant and fruity rosé.

Merlot: This is another classic grape that is associated with *Cabernet Sauvignon* in the Bordeaux region of France. Although similar to the latter grape, it usually produces a wine with softer tannins and hence, earlier drinkability. Displaying a dark blue-purple appearance when young, its flavor profile characteristically shows black cherries and ripe plums.

Nebbiolo: It is grown mostly in the northern hills of Piedmont, Italy, where it is the exclusive component in powerful and long-lived *Barolo, Barbaresco* and several other locally named Piedmontese red wines. Esteban Ferro of Bodegas de Santo Tomás first introduced it into the Valle de Guadalupe in the 1930's. In Piedmont, *Nebbiolo* produces huge wines with characteristic dark garnet color and with tannins that often take ten or twenty years to soften. But in time, the earthy aromas evolve to reveal aromas of dried plums, hints of violets and wood aging, while offering complex flavors of dried red stone fruit and good acidity. L.A. Cetto makes a popular *Reserva Limitada* version whose soft tannins permit its enjoyment after less than four years of bottle age.

Petite Sirah: **Long mistaken in California for** Petite Syrah **or** Syrah, **it now is identified as the** Durif, **a grape developed in the 1880's in France's Rhone Valley. During the 1970's in California, it was made in an inky black style that stained the teeth and puckered the palate of those who tasted the rustic young wine. In Baja the grape produces robust, balanced red wines with moderate tannins and more red stone fruit character.**

Syrah: **A grape variety associated with the Rhone region of France, it is a relatively new arrival to the Baja valleys. Although able to display several wine styles, the best are dry, dark red wines with a spicy peppery nose and good acid/tannin structure, capable of aging several years.** Syrah **also shows well in blends with** Cabernet Sauvignon.

Tempranillo: **Also known as** Valdepeñas, **it is primarily associated with wines of Spain's Rioja region. Several Baja producers have made wines from** Tempranillo, **sometimes in blends with other varietal grapes such as** Cabernet Sauvignon **and** Barbera. **While showing good ruby color, the wine's low acidity and its tendency to lose attractive fruit character relatively early, suggests a more promising future for the grape's use in blends than as the 100 percent varietal.**

Zinfandel: **This grape calls California its adopted home where more than fifty thousand acres are planted to this popular variety. As a wine, it is made in several styles although highly extracted fairly alcoholic versions are currently attracting consumer interest. Also of continued popularity is "White"** Zinfandel, **made by removing the purple grape skins immediately after crushing and fermenting the juice to produce a blush-style** slightly sweet and fruity aperitif wine. The robust red displays ripe berry aromas with acidic stone fruit and berry flavors, supported by moderate to significant mid tannins. In Baja this variety so far has produced rather rustic light-styled wines with less intense fruit character.

Part 4

Fests, Eats, Rests & Reads

Front cover of the Fiestas de la Vendimia 2002 guide for visitors.
(Courtesy: Asociación de Vinicultores)

Wine Festivals and Events

The annual harvest festivals are among the most effective promoters of Baja Mexican wine. These popular events regularly sell out in advance and the combined attendance numbers in the thousands. More festivals are springing up every year but the two major ones are these.

A grape stomping contest held during the annual all day and evening Fiesta Colores de Vendimia.

Fiestas de la Vendimia

The Ensenada Association of Viniculture organizes this harvest celebration, which usually is held during the first ten days of August. In addition to winery tours, an international wine contest, wine seminars, and cooking contests, a series of cultural events are held at the wineries. Ticket information is available from Viajes Damiana travel agency (tel. 011-52-646-178-3136, www.sdro.com/ensenadawines1). The events include:

Bodegas Santo Tomás: **Ensenada Street Fair**
Cavas Valmar: Mexican Delights: **Dinner and Music**
Casa Domecq: **New vintage celebration, Calafia Valley.**
Mogor-Badan: **Jazz Concert with Mediterranean Empanadas**
Viña de Liceaga: **Country Luncheon of Lamb and Music**
Monte Xanic: **Sunset Classical Music Concert with appetizers**
Chateau Camou: **Romantic Music Concert with hors d'ouvres**
Vinos Bibayoff: **Russian Memories: Country Luncheon & Russian Entertainment**
Adobe Guadalupe: **Gala Dinner and Wine Auction**
Casa de Piedra: Evening of Music, Dinner and Wine

Fiesta Colores de Vendimia

Organized by L.A. Cetto, it is held at their winery in the Valle de Guadalupe on one of the last weekends in August. This extravaganza starts around noon with a Mass to bless the grapes of the first harvest, accompanied frequently by a Mariachi band, followed by a grape-stomping contest, a tasting of all of Cetto's wines, lots of local cheese, a real bullfight in an authentic bullring, and a sit-down Mexican dinner held in a giant open-air pergola that offers perhaps the best view of the Valle de Guadalupe. After dark there's live music, dancing, more food and wine, and a concluding fireworks display. For ticket information contact L.A. Cetto (011-52-664-685-3031, Fax: 638-7121).

Where to Eat

O f course the best place to eat is as close to the wineries as possible. Since that is not always feasible, the partial list below includes several other eating locations that are my favorites. The principal requirements are that they serve wine-friendly locally influenced food and include Mexican wines on their wine lists.

Entrance to Restaurante LaJa, off Highway 3, at northern end of Valle de Guadalupe.

Valle de Guadalupe

1. Restaurante LaJa: **Km 83 Highway 3. Run by wife (La)-**
husband (Ja) team of Laura Reinert and Jair Tellez. With
training in San Francisco, New York and Mexico City, this
professional twosome prepare delicious *prix-fixe* French-style
menus that use local ingredients, which they serve in a high-
ceilinged wood-beamed dining room. Open 1:30-10 p.m. Thurs-
day-Sunday. Reservations recommended: laja@quatrodesign
.com or 646-155-2556.

2. Restaurante Mustafa: **Km 93, near the town of San**
Antonio de las Minas, on the left as entering Guadalupe
Valley from Ensenada. The friendly Moroccan owner serves
up simple but delicious lamb dishes and other Moroccan and
Mexican fare as well as acceptable homemade wine. Good
choice for informal lunch or dinner. Phone: 646-155-3095.

3. Restaurante Campestre Los Naranjos: **Km 82.5 on High-**
way 3. Very good native cuisine specializing in local quail
marinated in wine and spices. Inexpensive. Phone: 646-155-
2522.

Ensenada

1. El Rey Sol Restaurante: **Avenida López Mateos #1000, Zona Centro (646-178-1733). Long-established (over 55 years) restaurant, serving fine classic French cuisine & fresh local seafood dishes with a Mexican twist, & an extensive wine list including Baja wines. Breakfast/Lunch/Dinner.**

2. La Embotelladora Vieja: **666 Avenida Miramar, Zona Centro (Adjacent to Bodegas de Santo Tomás) (646-174-0807). Excellent gourmet Mexican/Mediterranean gastronomy and extensive Baja wine list. Dinner.**

3. La Esquina de Bodegas: **Avenida Miramar & 6th (across from Bodegas de Santo Tomás) (646-178-3557). Popular coffee bar and art gallery serving light meals and Santo Tomás wines. Breakfast/Lunch/Dinner.**

4. Sé De Vino: **Avenida Ruiz #138 (646-178-3433) (opposite Hussongs), Zona Central. Sophisticated wine & tapas bar, restaurant, & wine store. Lunch/Dinner.**

5. La Vendimia: **Avenida Riveroll #85, Zona Centro (646-174-0969). Restaurant, wine bar & wine shop, serving food & wines of Baja.**

6. Manzanilla: **Riveroll #122, Zona Centro (646-175-7073. Avant-garde regional Mexican cuisine & wines.**

Where to Rest

At the time of this writing the only recommended place within the Valley is Adobe Guadalupe. However, with increased development this is bound to change.

Adobe Guadalupe

Owners/Proprietors: **Don and Tru Miller**

Location: **Approximately 4 miles southwest of Francisco Zarco, past Chateau Camou. At the stop sign (adjacent to the Unidad Médica Familiar building) turn right and continue .5 mile more.**

Telephone: **949-863-9776 (USA), 011-52-646-155-2094 (Mexico)**

Fax: **949-955-1153 (USA), 011-52-646-155-2093 (Mexico)**

Email: **adobegpe@telnor.net**

Web Page: **http://www.adobeguadalupe.com**

Tru and Don Miller with two of their dogs in the central patio of their Adobe Guadalupe.

Where to Read More

1. *The Wines of America,* 3rd ed" by Leon Adams, McGraw-Hill, 1984. (A classic account of America's wine development and one of the first extensive and careful descriptions of Mexico's early wine industry.)

2. *Los Apuntes de un Cofrade,* (in Spanish) ("Notes of a Confraternity Member") by Héctor Arriola y Espinosa, privately printed (1000 copies), Ensenada, Baja California, 1997. (A personal but careful account of wines in Mexico by a long-time member of the *Confraternity of Wine of Baja California* [founded in 1986]. Also included are sections on wine-tasting protocol, and brief descriptions of other wine-producing areas of the world. May be found in some bookstores in Ensenada.)

3. *Vintage: The Story of Wine,* by Hugh Johnson, Simon & Schuster, NY, 1989. (The sections on the early wine industry in Spain and development of the wine industry in early California are useful in understanding the early wine development period in Mexico.)

4. *The Dominican Mission Frontier of Lower California,* by Peveril Meigs, 3rd, University of California Publications in Geography Vol. 7, 1935, Ed. C.O. Sauer & J.B. Leighly, U.C. Press, Berkeley, CA 1935. (The most authoritative and most cited work on this topic. Filled with field drawings of each mission site, along with fascinating descriptions based on earlier missionary journals. Out of print.)

5. *The Russian Colony of Guadalupe Molokans in Mexico,* by George W. Mohoff, privately published, 1995. (Interesting personal account of the history of the Russian Molokan Community with fascinating descriptions of their life style, daily activities, and conflict with the encroaching Mexican community.)

6. *The Oxford Companion to Wine,* by Jancis Robinson, Oxford University Press, Oxford, UK, 1994. (Fascinating and accurate mini-essays on all things related to wine. The essay on Mexican wine is out of date.)

7. *Terroir,* by James E. Wilson, University of California Press, Berkeley, CA, 1999. (A somewhat technical yet fascinating description and analysis of the environmental factors that influence how grapes grow and their effect on wine taste. The applications are primarily European and especially on France, but analogies can be made to other regions, such as Mexico.)

8. *Baja Handbook,* by Joe Cummings, Moon Publications Inc., Chico, CA, 1994. (Excellent guide to the roads and trails of Baja California, as well as an informative account of the history of the people who have occupied this region.)

9. *Baja California,* Automobile Club of Southern California, Costa Mesa, CA 92626. (Periodically updated, excellent travel guide and complement to Cummings' book.)

Glossary of Wine-Related Terms

The following terms may be found on labels or in literature about Mexican wine.

Acidez [Ah-see-dehs']...Acidity

Abocado ...Lightly Sweet

Afrutado [Ah-fru-ta'-do]...Fruity

Aguado [Ah-wah'-do]...Watery, Thin

Amargo [Ah-mar'-go]...Bitter

Añejamiento [Ah-nieh-haw-myen'-tow]...Ageing

Añejo [Ah-nieh'-hoe] ...Old, Old Vintage

Arcilloso [Ar-see-o'-so]...Clay-like (soil)

Áspero [Ah'-sper-o]...Sharp, Harsh

Aterciopelado [Ah-ter-see-o-peh-la'-do]...Velvety

Astringente [Ah-strin-hen'-teh]...Astringent

Azucar [Ah-soo-car']...Sugar

Badan [Bah-dahn']...Owner's name (see Mogor-Badan)

Barrica [Bah-rree'-ca]...Barrique, Cask

Barril [Bah-rreel']...Barrel, Keg

Bebida [Beh-bee'-da]...Beverage, Drink

Bibayoff [Bee'-by-off]...Owner's name (see Bibayoff Winery)

Blanco [Blan'co]...White

Boca [Bow'ca]...Mouth

Bodega [Bo-deh'-ga]...Wine cellar, Winery

Bordalés [Bor-da-lehs']...from Bordeaux

Borgoñona [Bor-go-ni-own'-ah]...Burgundian

Bosque [Bows'-keh]...Forest, Woods

Botella [Bo-tay'-a]...Bottle

Burdeos [Boor-day'-ohs]...Bordeaux [wine], Burgundy [color]

Caja [Caw'-haw]...Case, Box

Calidad [Ca-li-dad']...Quality

Caliente [Cal-i-en'-teh]...Hot

Caluroso [Cal-u-ro'-so]...Hot, Warm (alcohol)

Camou [Ca-moo']...Owner's name (see Chateau Camou)

Carnoso [Car-no'-so]...Fleshy, Meaty

Cava [Cah'-vah]...Cellar, Winery

Cedro [Sed'-dro]...Cedar

Cepa [Seh'-pa]...Rootstock, Variety

Cerrado [Seh-rrah'-do]...Closed

Cetto [Cheh'toh]...Owner's name (see L.A. Cetto)

Clima [Clee'-ma]...Climate

Colorante [Coe-low-ran'-tey]...Coloring

Copa [Coe'-pa]...Wine glass

Copa flauta [Coe'-pa flou'-ta]...Champagne flute

Corcho [Cor'-cho]...Cork

Corto [Cor'-to]...Short, Small glass

Cosecha [Coe-seh'-cha]...Harvest

Crianza [Cree-ahn'-sa]...Breeding

Cuerpo [Quer'-po]...Body

Débil [Deh'-bil]...Weak

Degustación [Deh-goo-stah-see-own']...Wine Tasting

Dulce [Dool'-say] ...Sweet

Duro [Doo'-ro] ...Hard, Harsh

Embotellado [Em-bow-tay-ah'-dow] ...Bottled

Espumosa [Es-poo-mow'-sah] ...Bubbling, Sparkling

Etiqueta [Eht-ee-ket'-a] ...Bottle Label

Finura [Fee-noo'-rah] ...Fineness, Subtlety

Franco [Fran'-co] ...Forward, Open

Fresa [Freh'-sah] ...Strawberry

Frio [Free'-o] ...Cold

Fruta [Froo'-tah] ...Fruit

Gobelet [Go-beh-let'] ...A goblet-shaped form of vineyard
    trellising

Gusto [Goo'-stow] ...Taste

Hecho en Mexico [Eh'-chow en Meh'hi-co] ...Made in Mexico

Jóven [Ho'-ven] ...Young, youthful

Jugo [Hoo'-go] ...Juice

Lagar [La-gar'] ...Winepress

Leyvadura [Leh-vah-doo'-ra] ...Yeast

Lías [Lee'-ahs] ...Lees

Liceaga [Lee-seh-ah'-ga] ...Owner's name (see Vinos Liceaga)

Ligero [Lee-heh'-ro] ...Slight, Faint (color)

Limitada [Li-mi-tah'-dah] ...Limited

Madurado [Mah-doo-rah'-do] ...Mature, Ripe

Mantequilla [Man-teh-key'-ah] ...Butter

Manzana [Man-sah'-na] ...Apple

Marbete [Mar-beh'-teh] ...Tax stamp

Mediano [Meh-di-ah'-no] ...Medium

Medio [Meh'-di-o] ...Middle

Mezcla [Mes'-clah] ...Mixture, Blend

Miel [Mee-ehl'] ...Honey

Mosto [Mow'-sto] ...Must (juice of the fresh grape)

Monte [Mon'teh]...Mountain, Mount

Naranja [Nahran'ha]...Orange

Nuevo [Neweh'vo]...New

Obscuro [Ovscoo'ro]...Dark, Obscure

Olfato [Olefah'to]...Olfactory, Sense of Smell

Olores [Ohloh'rais]...Odors, Scents

Pan [Pahn]...Bread

Picante [Peecahn'teh]...Piquant, Sharp, Tart

Piedra [Peeay'drah]...Stone

Plano [Plah'no]...Flat

Pleno [Pleh'no]...Full

Por Ciento [Por Syen'to]...Percent

Pungente [Punhen'tey]...Pungency

Redondo [Rehdon'do]...Round

Reserva Privada [Rehsair'vah Preevah'da]...Private Reserve

Reservado [Rehsairvah'doh]...Special or Vintage Wine

Rico [Ree'coh]...Rich

Roble [Row'bleh]...Oak

Rojo [Row'ho]...Red

Rosado [Rowsaw'do]...Rosé

Sabor [Sawbor']...Flavor

Sacacorchos [Sawcacor'chos]...Corkscrew

Salado [Sawla'do]...Salty

Seco [Seh'co]...Dry, Dried

Sedoso [Sehdow'so]...Silky-Smooth

Semilla [Sehmee'a]...Seed

Sobre las Lías [Sow'bray las Lee'ahs]...Sur Lie

Suavidad [Swaveedad']...Softness

Suelo [Sweh'lo]...Soil

Tánica [Tahn'ica]...Tannic

Tierra [Tyeh'-rra]...Earth, Soil

Tinto [Teen'-to]...Red, Tint

Tonel [Tow-nel']...Large Barrel

Tosco [Tos'-co]...Rough, Coarse (tannin)

Tostado [Tow-stah'-do]...Toasted, Yellow-Brown

Uva [Oo'-va]...Grape

Variedad [Var-yeh-dad']...Variety

Vaso de Vino [Vah'-so de Vee'no]...Glass of Wine

Vendimia [Ven-dee'-mya]...Harvest, Vintage

Verde [Ver'-deh]...Green

Vid [Veed]...Vine, Grapevine

Viñedos [Vee-ni-eh'-dos]...Vineyards

Vino [Vee'-no]...Wine

Vivo [Vee'-vo]...Alive

Xanic [Zhan-eek']... "1st flower after the rain" (see Monte Xanic)

Index